D1559551

209 BIG PROGRAMMING IDEAS FOR SMALL BUDGETS

ALA Editions purchases fund advocacy, awareness,
and accreditation programs for library professionals worldwide.

Published in partnership
with The Association for
Rural & Small Libraries

209 BIG PROGRAMMING IDEAS FOR SMALL BUDGETS

CHELSEA PRICE

ALA
Editions
CHICAGO   2021

CHELSEA PRICE has been the library director in Meservey, Iowa, since 2015. She has presented at the Kids First Conference in Des Moines, Iowa, and the Association for Rural & Small Libraries Conference in Springfield, Illinois, and she presented webinars for the Programming Librarian website and the Wild Wisconsin Winter Web Conference. She also writes regularly for the *Programming Librarian* blog. In her spare time, Price and her husband love to volunteer at animal shelters all over the Midwest, and they have four senior rescue dogs of their own.

© 2021 by Chelsea Price

Extensive effort has gone into ensuring the reliability of the information in this book; however, the publisher makes no warranty, express or implied, with respect to the material contained herein.

ISBN: 978-0-8389-4811-8 (paper)

Library of Congress Cataloging-in-Publication Data

Names: Price, Chelsea, author.
Title: 209 big programming ideas for small budgets / Chelsea Price.
Description: Chicago : ALA Editions, 2021. | Includes bibliographical references and index. | Summary: "This book will help you plan programs on a small budget and will provide tips for smart fundraising and grant-seeking opportunities"—Provided by publisher.
Identifiers: LCCN 2020029649 | ISBN 9780838948118 (paperback)
Subjects: LCSH: Libraries—Activity programs. | Small libraries.
Classification: LCC Z716.33 .P75 2021 | DDC 027—dc23
LC record available at https://lccn.loc.gov/2020029649

Cover design by Kim Thornton.

Text design in the Chaparral, Gotham, and Bell Gothic typefaces.

♾ This paper meets the requirements of ANSI/NISO Z39.48-1992 (Permanence of Paper).

Printed in the United States of America

25 24 23 22 21   5 4 3 2 1

Dedicated to my mom and dad,
who can finally stop bugging me
about writing a book.

Contents

Preface

Adventures in Tiny Librarianship

I CAME BY MY WORK IN LIBRARIES NATURALLY—MY MOM WAS also the director of a tiny library. She was in that role for about 15 years, and *her* mom was a school librarian from age 40 to 80! I grew up in the library, and my mom let me work there throughout high school, shelving books and answering the phone. I do *not* have a library science degree; I have a bachelor's degree in psychology, which comes in handy while working at the library, to be honest.

I was hired as library director in the tiny, rural town of Meservey, Iowa, in early 2015. The Meservey Public Library had been without a director for several months, so I was tossed into the position with very little training, and I had to find my footing very quickly. I managed to get the hang of it, and I immediately felt right at home. I realized pretty quickly that I was meant to work in a tiny library.

The town of Meservey is only about 1.5 square miles in area, and the population hovers right around 250. The school there closed in the early 1980s, and the nearest school in our district is now nearly a half hour away. Meservey doesn't have a gas station, community center, or bank—though it does have a church, a fire station, a post office, a bar, and my little library.

The library is housed in a one-room building. We are open just twenty hours a week and I have one library assistant, without whom I don't think I could function. We don't have a Friends group, and we have an annual budget of approximately $30,000 . . . and that includes materials and employee pay.

We have to stretch our dollars as far as they can possibly go to pull off great programs.

Despite our budget limitations, we have managed to more than triple our attendance numbers over the past three years. That's not to say that all of our programs are successful—we have ranged anywhere from zero attendees all the way up to 400 at our annual carnival. In a town like ours, the programs we offer are just as important (I'd venture to say maybe even more so) as the materials we offer. We have to be creative when it comes to getting the most bang for our programming buck, and many of our programs have been possible thanks to the generosity and support of the community.

Many Iowa libraries are very similar to mine—about 95 percent of them are considered small, and nearly 80 percent are considered rural.[1] The majority of Iowa libraries are single-service outlets, which means that most of us aren't part of a library system—we are on our own, which creates a lack of connection between libraries. I hope that this book will help those of you who are working in similar libraries and help you feel a little less alone in your efforts to create amazing programs.

I am not an expert; I want to make that clear before we get started. I am just a library director—who still doesn't quite know what she's doing—who has managed to stumble into a magical and wonderful job, pulling off a few great programs along the way. I hope this book will inspire you and that you finish reading it feeling excited about your job. Happy reading, and happy programming.

FIGURE 0.1 / Meservey Library

NOTE

1. Deanne W. Swan, Justin Grimes, and Timothy Owens, "The State of Small and Rural Libraries in the United States," Institute of Museum and Library Services Research Brief No. 5 (September 2013).

Introduction

Small Libraries, Big Hearts

RURAL LIBRARIANSHIP MIGHT SEEM UNUSUAL TO SOME IN THE library world. If you're a librarian in a small, rural library, you are probably aware that library school didn't prepare you for this. Things just work differently in tiny libraries. There was no class on getting along with a difficult city council member or how to deal with a neighbor whose tractor takes up too much space in your parking lot. You probably didn't learn much about comforting a crying child, creating programs with absolutely no budget, or bringing a sense of community to your geographically isolated town. No, there's no degree training for any of that.

Being a small, rural librarian often means you wear all of the hats, and there aren't too many jobs like that. You are the computer tech, the custodian, and the day care provider. You cover outreach, youth services, and adult services. You advertise, keep the books, and do the landscaping. You help create resumes, conduct research, and tie children's shoes. And some of you are doing all of that alone. (Let's have a quick round of applause for all of the solo librarians out there!)

The definition of a "small" library can vary pretty wildly, but it is generally agreed that a small library serves a population of less than 25,000, and "rural" just means that you are far away from any urban area. Many of you reading this book probably think a population of 25,000 is huge compared to your community (and I'm right there with you). Small and rural libraries make up about 80.5 percent of all the public libraries in the United States,[1] so there's a lot of them out there. The sheer numbers of these small libraries throughout the country speak volumes about the value that communities place on their services.

Public libraries have changed dramatically over the years, and nowadays they offer so much more than just books to borrow. Libraries are more involved in their communities than ever before—they are true community centers, the nucleus of the town, the "anchor" of the community. There may not be a restaurant in your town, and there are probably no shopping malls; maybe there's no grocery store, gas station, or even a school . . . but there's usually a church, and there's *always* a library. The library is *it* for many communities; it is often the only source of free WI-FI, the only public meeting space, and the only option for free entertainment within 20 or 30 miles. It's all on you.

The fact that libraries continue to grow despite the struggles they are facing is a true testament to your ability to change and evolve. As the needs of your community change, so will your library. This goes to show how resilient libraries are and how relevant they have always been to rural life; they continue to provide invaluable resources to their communities, no matter how tiny and isolated those may be. Rural libraries continue to raise the bar with the breadth of the programs they offer, and no matter how tight their budgets get, they still have a huge impact on their community.

It's true that small libraries face a lot of challenges, and even hardships. The never-ending dwindling of budgets, for one. A lack of staff, of time, of resources, of space. It is rare for tiny libraries to be able to give their staff paid vacations or health benefits. You may feel stretched thin at times, and that you're fighting a losing battle when trying to advocate for your library. Perhaps one of the most difficult things about working in a small library is that there is so little division between your work life and your home life. It can feel, sometimes, like you're never off the job, that you always have to be "on." This is true, in a sense. In a tiny town, you are the library, and the library is you.

But I think you will find, while reading this book, that little libraries can be powerful libraries, and what you don't have in space or funding, you can make up for in spades with innovation, creativity, and oh my gosh, *so* much heart.

You probably know almost every patron by name, and you even know what authors to recommend to your regulars. (James Patterson. It's always James Patterson.) Your patrons have gotten to know you as well—heck, they probably even know your dad and maybe even the name of your dog—and they bring you fresh vegetables from their garden. You receive compliments and words of appreciation far more than you receive complaints or negativity, and you probably feel some sense of safety, knowing that in small towns, the "neighborhood watch" is always active.

While your library's value to your community is indisputable, you probably face quite a challenge when it comes to funding. However, you're also adaptable, clever, and great at forming partnerships in your community (or you will be once you've read this book). You take pride in being able to offer your patrons a safe and welcoming space where they can gather together without ever having to spend any money. You may never again have such an opportunity to make such an indelible mark on a community.

This book will lead you through planning programs on a tiny budget by way of thriftiness, some out-of-the-box ideas, and partnerships. You will learn about smart fundraising and grant-seeking, and you'll find tips on staying passionate while working in a library. Along the way, you'll read about programs done by other libraries like yours around the country (even a few from Canada, our neighbors to the north) that have done a lot with a little—not all of these libraries are considered "small," but all of the programs included here should be easy to replicate in a library of any size. Keep up the good fight, and let this book guide you on your way to program-planning greatness!

NOTE

1. Deanne W. Swan, Justin Grimes, and Timothy Owens, "The State of Small and Rural Libraries in the United States," Institute of Museum and Library Services Research Brief No. 5 (September 2013).

1

The Power of Passive Programs

WHILE WORKING IN A SMALL LIBRARY IS A HIGHLY REWARDING experience, it can be overwhelming sometimes. Library budgets are frequently getting cut, and you've probably experienced the struggle of trying to make ends meet when it comes to programming. However, you're still expected to keep churning out program after program, regardless of how low your budgets go. It's not always easy. Whether you feel like you're in over your head when it comes to program planning, or you just need some easy ideas that don't require a lot of time or effort, passive programming is there for you!

WHAT ARE PASSIVE PROGRAMS?

"Passive" programs are so-called because they are temporary, self-directed activities that patrons can interact with at their own time and at their own choosing. These programs usually require little or no supervision and cost very little to implement. Passive programs are often forgotten about because they're less "flashy" than regular programming. However, they are often just as effective (sometimes even more so) than your regularly scheduled programs, they still count in your programming numbers, and they make for

5 Reasons Why Passive Programming Is a Must-Do

1. **It's more flexible.** Patrons can enjoy your passive programming on any day at any time.

2. **It's cheap.** Passive programming is almost always very budget friendly.

3. **It increases interactions.** Whether the interactions are between caregiver and child or between you/staff members and patrons, these are little conversations that might not have happened otherwise.

4. **It makes for great marketing.** Patrons and potential donors love to see how much participation and interaction there are at the library.

5. **It's fun!** Passive programming is just fun, for patrons and staff alike. Patrons enjoy the activity, while the staff enjoys the low-cost, low-effort aspect of it—it's a win-win situation!

great photos and social media posts. Plus, they require very minimal time, energy, and supervision by library staff . . . so what is there to lose?

The possibilities for passive programming (also called stealth or individual programming) are practically endless. You could take it online for some social media challenges such as shelfies (book shelf selfies) or Bookfaces (photos of the patron posed with a book covering part of their face to line up with the cover art—this is not an easy concept to explain, but Google it and you won't be disappointed). You could print out a book Bingo sheet to encourage patrons to read across genres and age ranges, or you could shred a few pages of a popular book—a discarded copy, of course—and put it in a jar to see if patrons can guess the title. Another popular idea is to have an "I Spy" wall or bulletin board, filled with random objects—whether they're physical items or just printed on a piece of paper—and a little rhyme to encourage patrons to find specific items among them.

Your passive programs could also be seasonal. You could have patrons pre-vote for the Academy Awards and give a small prize to anyone with a winning ballot. Celebrate National Random Acts of Kindness Day (February 17) by having a jar full of ideas—give someone a compliment, pick up a piece of litter, cook for someone—and encourage your patrons to pick one and follow through with the act. During Children's Book Week, print out silhouettes of popular children's book characters and see if your young patrons can guess who's who. Use your imagination, and you'll find that just about any holiday or event can be a great inspiration for a passive program.

Steal These Ideas!

Set up scavenger hunts. Hide things around your library and let your young patrons hunt for them. This sounds simple, but kids get such a kick out of finding hidden items! For example, hide gold coins around the library on St. Patrick's Day and offer a small prize to anyone who can hunt one down. Or during Children's Book Week, hide photos of popular characters around the kids' area. The hunts can be themed like this, or they can be completely random.

Add a Lego to the tower. Each time a patron checks out an item, let them add a Lego brick to the tower and watch it grow and grow. You could also take this idea and apply it to something else, like a sticky-note art piece or a cardboard tube sculpture. It's fun to watch a project grow in size over the month or the summer. This can be especially fun during your summer reading program, and you could even use it as a reading incentive.

Think up fun whiteboard polls. Do your patrons like books or movies better? Are they introverts or extroverts? Do they prefer savory or sweet snacks? Put a weekly question up on a whiteboard and let your community vote. Not only is this a fun way to interact with patrons, it also enables you to get to know them a bit better. You can also ask open-ended questions, as well as questions that can help you better serve them as a library, such as "What program would you like to attend?" or "Do you prefer paper books or e-books?"

Create your own brackets for March Madness (book character vs. book character). This is a very popular idea at many libraries—rather than worrying about NCAA basketball teams, put up brackets on a bulletin board or whiteboard pitting different books or book characters against one another. Will *Hunger Games* beat out *Harry Potter* for best book series? Can Elephant beat out Piggie for most popular children's book character? Let your patrons vote on these choices, and talk it up on social media.

Display patrons' collections (geode collection, postage stamps, etc.). Many libraries feature a different patron collection each month. This is a great way for your community to get to know one another a little better—who knew your mayor had such an awesome toy car collection? This also makes for great posts on social media.

Put together a giving tree or library wish list. During the holidays or all year round, display a giving tree (whether it's a real tree or a bulletin board one) with different wishes the library has written on each leaf. If your library is in need of cleaning supplies, write that on a leaf. You can also write things that are out of the library's reach, like a robotics kit or a tablet—you never know what people might be generous enough to give.

Leave out crafts or a puzzle for patrons to play with at their leisure. It will be difficult to get a good idea of how many people have participated, but fun nonetheless.

Curate a patron art gallery or Post-It note art gallery. Put out a call for your patrons to contribute to a library art gallery. Cover a window or wall with their creations as they come in. If you'd like to make this into a partnership, contact an art teacher in your school district and see if she would be interested in participating.

Put out a mural for patrons to color. Put a giant coloring sheet over a table or wall with a container of crayons or colored pencils nearby. Your patrons can be artists at their leisure, all contributing to a giant community art piece.

IDEAS IN ACTION

Choose Kind Cardmaking

LAURA ARNHOLD, Upper Merion Township Library,
King of Prussia, Pennsylvania

Every community can use a little more kindness and love, and our Choose Kind Cardmaking program helps us in two ways. First, we're offering a program for our patrons, and two, we're brightening the lives of the people in our community by sending out these sweet cards. The kids get so excited to make a card. We usually put out a simple sign that says they can make one card to take home and share with someone they love, and make an additional card to support our community. What makes Choose Kind Cardmaking so great is that it can easily be adapted to fit almost any library. It can be either passive, with supplies set up at a table in the library, or it can be a scheduled program for kids and families to attend. The supplies are very inexpensive.

Our library has offered this program a number of times, each time reaching out to different groups in our community—senior citizens in assisted living facilities, the public safety department of our township, students as they gear up for finals, and soldiers fighting overseas. We offer it as a program in our children's department, but this could easily be a program for all ages in a public library. Even the time of year can change—it's a great program to fill in between scheduled events or as a lead-up event for a holiday, or to support World Kindness Day. We like being able to teach kids how to "be the change" and positively affect their own community.

Creation Station

HALEY LETCH, Stirling-Rawdon Public Library,
Stirling, Ontario, Canada

At the Stirling-Rawdon Public Library in Stirling, Ontario, we took an unused desk and an empty corner and turned them into a makerspace area. We serve a population of approximately 5,000, and we have a small budget that forces us to be creative in order to make it stretch as far as possible. Our Creation Station is a low-tech, craft-making station that is unstaffed. We have a different theme each month. In the past year, some of the things we've done were a Snowflake Discovery Station, Pipe Cleaner Creations, Magazine Poetry, Valentine's Day Cards, Whirlybirds, Christmas Ornaments, and a Santa Letter-Writing Station. One month we even just put out some random craft supplies and challenged kids to use their imaginations to just make something, anything they wanted.

The idea with the Creation Station is to just put out craft materials with a general theme and let kids use their imaginations to create something. Sometimes I will put out some books on the theme to encourage kids or parents to read more about the topic, or to get ideas about what to make. I might also include some "fun facts" on the topic. There is little instruction or supervision involved. The kids also have the choice to take home what they've made or leave it on the bulletin board for everyone to see. In our library, there isn't always someone working in the children's department, so this makes it difficult to get an accurate idea of the number of participants each month, but we generally see 20–30 kids use the station each month—sometimes more, sometimes less, depending on the time of year (summer is more popular) and what the theme for the month is. We're a small library, so these are really good numbers for us. The kids range in age from 2 to 13.

FIGURE 1.1

Snowflake-themed Creation Station

Overall, the Creation Station has cost the library very little. Generally, we use craft supplies we already have. These might be materials left over from other programs, or something that has been donated for us to use. Occasionally, I will take advantage of interlibrary loan if we don't have a lot of books on the topic, so that people can learn more about that topic. I try not to purchase anything at all and will instead go into our craft supplies to see what we have a lot of, and then search Google or Pinterest for ideas on what we can do with cotton balls, pipe cleaners, yarn, or whatever we have, and then go from there.

The response from the community has been overwhelmingly positive. When we post these things on our social media pages or even if people just wander in, we get a lot of people commenting about "what a great idea this is," "it's so nice to have things for kids to do in the library," and so on. The kids and parents seem to like having something to do when they visit the library, and it makes them stay longer too!

2

Thrifty and Nifty

WHILE MANY LIBRARIES' PROGRAMMING BUDGETS ARE TIGHT, some libraries have no programming budget at all, and have to rely only on fundraisers, Friends groups (if they have one), grants, and sheer ingenuity to make their programs happen. Without financial assistance, many libraries can't hire performers or speakers, and they can't always offer elaborate crafts and tasty snacks at every program. They must scrimp, save, and brainstorm ingenious ways to pull off amazing programs on little or no money.

This is not easy. But it's possible. Your library can create and execute innovative and memorable programs, even with little or no wiggle room in your programming budget. In this chapter, we'll explore all kinds of fun ideas for programs for all ages, and you'll learn some clever ways to get the most bang for your programming buck.

LOW-COST PROGRAM IDEAS

Librarians are always looking for great program ideas that are budget-friendly and easy. The following ideas are simple and won't put much of a dent in your programming budget.

5 Tips for Bringing Patrons in the Door

1. **Provide food.** If you feed them, they will come!

2. **Include hands-on activities.** Everyone enjoys interactive activities where they can really get their hands dirty.

3. **Offer new and different experiences.** Teach attendees to do something new or give them an experience they may never have had otherwise.

4. **Make it FREE.** Free is always good and always appreciated!

5. **Share your passion and enthusiasm.** Chances are, if you love it, other people in your community will love it too.

Steal These Ideas!

Hold Lego challenges. Host a Lego party where the attendees have Lego challenges and build specific patterns as quickly as they can. Make some life-size Legos out of cardboard boxes, colored paper, and colored paper plates, and put them aside as décor or let patrons build with them. An easy snack that doubles as an activity is edible Legos—graham crackers frosted with primary colored frosting and topped with M&Ms as the Lego "studs."

Concoct some slime. Make fluffy slime, sticky slime, runny slime, and more, from items you probably have on hand. Tons of recipes can be found online, and slime is often made with items you have (or patrons might have) lying around the house. Contact solution, cornstarch, glue (*so much glue!*), and shaving cream are a few of the more popular ingredients. Chances are, your young patrons won't even need instructions—they'll see the ingredients and go to town.

Create a string art piece. String art consists of pleasing arrangements of colored string (or yarn, thread, or wire) strung between points to form complex geometric patterns. The "points" consists of nails hammered into a baseboard that has been covered with black velvet. String art is an inexpensive way to create cool, unique art for your home, and it makes a great adult program. You can either do a register-first program and print out pattern templates for each registered attendee beforehand, or you can just print out several templates for each attendee to choose from when they arrive. Small wooden baseboards (or plaques) can be purchased in bulk for a reasonable price on Amazon. Watch a tutorial on YouTube first, but this is a fairly simple craft to do, and each attendee will leave with a personalized piece of art to display in their home.

Host a Pinterest party. Pinterest parties are low-key gatherings where adults come together to craft, eat snacks, and connect. If there is a specific item you have a surplus of, look it up on Pinterest. For this example, let's use mason jars. Type in "crafts using mason jars" on Pinterest, and you'll find projects like ombre glitter mason jars, mason jar tissue dispensers, and decoupaged leaf mason jars. Pick two or three projects that you have most of the materials for, and print out tutorials for each attendee to have at the party. If you have time, do the projects yourself beforehand so you'll have an example and can provide help to attendees. Have all of the materials handy for your patrons, and let them craft and converse! If you want to get more into the Pinterest theme, host a "Pinterest potluck," where attendees bring a dish they've made using a Pinterest recipe to share with the group.

Become a mad scientist with mason jars. Speaking of mason jars, there is *so much* that can be done with them that would make great programs! You can turn them into snow globes, calming glitter jars, and so much more. One of the most popular activities with older kids is mason jar science experiments. Many of these can be done with items that you have on hand: glitter, food coloring, shaving cream, baking soda, vinegar, and vegetable oil. And a hot tip: cleaned-out spaghetti sauce jars with the labels peeled off are basically mason jars!

Paint rocks. Art projects are often pretty low-cost, but you can't get much cheaper than rock painting! If you're in a rural, farming community, see if any local farmers have decent-sized rocks to donate. Then gather your paints and make sure you have sealant to put over each rock so the paint will stay vibrant. Let patrons make whatever designs they'd like on their rocks. If you're inspired to do so, do a "kindness rocks" campaign around your library by painting positive messages and pictures on each rock and hiding them in and around the library building.

Stamp with fruits and vegetables. Fruit and veggie stamping is a low-cost, fun art project. Pick out fruits and veggies that have various internal textures to see what each will look like when stamped on a sheet of paper—cucumbers, apples, broccoli, and potatoes all work well. Slice the fruit or vegetable in half, dip the bottom of these "stamps" in paint, then get to stamping! You can also cut shapes into apples or potatoes to add interest to your project.

Craft with Perler beads. Perler beads have recently become a huge trend again—older kids and teens love making fun shapes and designs with them, like emoji keychains and Pokémon characters. The beads are very reasonably priced, and you just need parchment paper and an iron to melt them into shapes.

Decorate the library's windows. Young patrons love to feel helpful. They're often eager to "help" you with decorating the library, so turn that opportunity into a program and have a window-decorating party! This can be especially fun around homecoming or a big sports event in the community. Window crayons are fairly cheap and are easy to wash off later.

Host a DIY spa night. A DIY spa night is a great idea for tweens, teens, and even adults. You can make this as expensive or low-cost as you'd like. There are plenty of recipes out there that could easily get expensive—buying individual lip balm containers, buying beeswax, including essential oils . . . these could all add up fast. But you could also keep it super simple by making face masks out of common ingredients like oatmeal, yogurt, and honey, infusing water with different fruits and vegetables, or putting cucumber slices over your eyes.

Host a teen taste-test program. Teen patrons will almost always show up where there is free food, so why not do a taste-test program? You can do this with many different items: soda, chocolate, Oreos . . . the list goes on. Have each attendee guess what brand they're eating/drinking, rate which one they like the best, and then reveal what they were sampling at the end. It's fun and easy, and they go home with full stomachs!

Play "Minute-to-Win-It" games. There are *so* many Minute to Win It games out there that you could do a weekly program and never run out of ideas. These games are basically races to complete an action within sixty seconds, and they're most popular with the tween age group. Search "Minute to Win It" on YouTube to learn the general rules of the game. Here are some popular ones:

> *Separation Anxiety*: Sort a giant bag of M&Ms or Skittles into cups by color.
> *Marshmallow Chopsticks*: Using only chopsticks, move mini marshmallows from one place to another.
> *Face the Cookie*: Tilt your head back and place a small cookie (Oreo, Chips Ahoy) on your forehead. Try to get the cookie into your mouth using only the muscles in your face.

Incorporate sensory bins. Sensory play for infants and toddlers is necessary for their development. To create a sensory bin, fill an empty tote bag with just about anything you can think of—pasta or dried beans tend to be the "base" that's used most often. Hide other objects inside, and have kids dig with spoons, cups, and hands to find the hidden objects. You can also fill the bin with slime, sand, Play-Doh, or shaving cream if you're willing to get a little messy!

Create sensory bottles. Fill empty bottles with water and a little bit of clear glue (the glue will make the water seem to move in "slow motion" as you move the bottle). Then add liquid watercolors, sequins, glitter, shells, googly eyes, and any other small objects you'd like. Hot-glue the cap of the bottle shut to avoid any leaks. Young kids are entranced by the movement of the objects inside!

Do some gravity painting. Collect empty spray bottles, eyedroppers, and sponges, and let your young attendees test out different methods of gravity painting; that is, spraying or brushing paint on sheets of paper hung vertically. Before starting, hang pieces of recycled paper from a table, and add small amounts of watercolor to some water. The more water you use, the drippier your paint will be. This is a very messy program, so do it outside or put a tarp down on the floor inside. Not only will the kids be using their creativity, they can also see gravity working in front of their eyes as the paint drips down the paper.

Host a bubble party. Put on some music, grab your bubble machine, put out containers of bubble solution and wands of all different sizes, and let the kids go to town! You can also make your own bubble solution using water, dish soap, and corn syrup. If you want to extend the theme, grab some bubble wrap from any packages you've received recently, and let the kids dance and stomp all over it to pop the bubbles. What kid wouldn't love that?

IDEAS IN ACTION

"The Office" Trivia Night

CHELSEA PRICE, Meservey Public Library, Meservey, Iowa

I never thought my library could pull off a trivia night, but I love the TV show *The Office* so much that I honestly wanted to do a trivia night—more for myself than for anyone else. So I decided to go for it. I was happily surprised when we ended up with thirty-six very happy attendees. This was by far my favorite event to plan for and decorate; there were little references to the show all over the library, and the attendees had a great time finding all of them.

For the trivia quiz, I made a simple PowerPoint slideshow for the questions, one question per slide, using our smart TV to put the slideshow up on the big screen. Each team got a whiteboard and marker, so there was no shouting out answers. The attendees came in costume, which made for some great photos. Everyone had a blast.

The decorations and props were simple and cost next to nothing. I provided some snacks, all of which referenced *The Office* in some way, and we gave

FIGURE 2.1 / All of our costumed *Office* trivia participants

away several prizes. The snacks were low-cost—I asked for a discount at a local bakery and received half off soft baked pretzels!—but the prizes cost more than I would usually spend. I purchased a few smaller things from Redbubble—posters, stickers, and magnets—and a couple of larger prizes, including a Dwight bobblehead and a blue teapot (if you know, you know). To try and balance the cost of the prizes, I put out a donation bucket at the front desk during the event. To my surprise, at the end of the night we had around $120 in there, which was more than enough to pay for those prizes—a sure sign of a successful program!

FREE PROGRAM IDEAS

Not much is better than a low-cost program . . . except a program that's totally *free*! The ideas below can be pulled off on a $0 budget (besides staff time, of course). Though it's possible to turn these free ideas into low-cost ideas—by offering snacks, buying props, and so on—it's totally doable to hold these programs for no cost at all.

Steal These Ideas!

Host a Read a Million Minutes event. Did your school ever do Read a Million Minutes? On the last day of that reading program at my school, we would all bring in our sleeping bags, our favorite books, and a few snacks to eat. We would spend the whole afternoon in our sleeping bags just reading and eating, and it was absolute heaven. Why not re-create that—or something like it—at the library? Bring in a bunch of blankets (or have patrons bring their own, if you prefer; same with the snacks) and sprawl out on the floor, eating . . . and reading furiously. A variation of this is a family fort night, where families build forts around the library using furniture and blankets and then read books inside them. If you'd like to further pursue the "summer camp" theme, you could provide s'mores in a cup (teddy grahams, mini marshmallows, and chocolate chips), flashlights, and scary stories . . . or have a free event by encouraging attendees to bring their own snacks.

Set up book dominoes. If you don't mind the cleanup (or you have a very patient shelver), you could have a book dominoes program, where you line up books on their ends in various patterns and then knock them over. It sounds simple, but search it on YouTube—some libraries make superintricate designs with their books, and it's mesmerizing to watch!

Hold a mini-golf tournament. Host a miniature golf tournament in the library using books as barriers and obstacles. To avoid spending money, ask around in the community to see if you can borrow some putters and golf balls.

Hold a library speed dating night. Have you ever heard of library speed dating? No, it's not dating to find a potential mate—although I suppose you could do that as a program, too—it's dating to find a potential book to read! Each attendee brings three books they loved to share with the group. They can talk a bit about what each book is about and why they loved it so much, and then move on to the next person. Each attendee should go home with a bunch of new titles in their minds to add to their "to be read" list.

Host a local history night. A local history night is a fun, nostalgic program that doesn't cost the library anything at all. Invite long-standing community members to bring in their old photos or scrapbooks from years ago and share stories and memories with other attendees. It's always so interesting to see what your community used to be like.

Swap recipes at a potluck. Have each attendee make their favorite dish to bring in and share with other patrons, bringing along the written recipe. Recipes can be swapped, and all attendees can go home with some new dishes to cook. If you'd like, you can even collect the recipes yourself and create a library cookbook, which could possibly be sold later on as a fundraiser!

Host a dance party. Young kids love to dance. Put on some kid-appropriate music, add some bubbles and props (shaker eggs, scarves, etc.), and you've got yourself a good time. Dance parties or preschool proms are almost always a huge hit. Try to get the parents involved, too, and don't be afraid to make a fool of yourself—kids can smell fear, and they will start feeling weird if they can tell that *you* feel weird. You can even put on some dance videos—the *Tooty Ta Song* and *Shake Your Sillies Out* are some popular ones (if you haven't heard of these, consider yourself lucky). If you've requested that parents and kids dress up for the event (whether it's in their Sunday best or in 1950s sock hop gear), think about putting up a photo booth backdrop and making some props so parents can take photos with their kids.

Host a video game tournament. If your library doesn't have a video game system, ask around and see if you have a patron who is an avid gamer and might be willing to bring in their collection for a program. Video games can keep kids entertained for hours, and game tournaments are sure to be a hit. Avoid violent video games or games rated "Mature." *Mario Kart* is popular with all age groups! Set a timer to give each player fifteen-minute turns so as to avoid arguments.

Teach a yoga or exercise class. This can be as easy as pulling up a YouTube video. There are so many great yoga/Zumba/pilates videos out there that you don't need to search around for an instructor to teach a class. Just search for beginner videos, and then you can increase the difficulty level as your group's skill level improves.

Do some karaoke or lip-syncing. If your patrons are too shy to do full-out karaoke, consider hosting a Lip Sync Battle, based on the popular TV show.

Make a rule that there will be no inappropriate songs allowed, and each performer will be limited to 3.5 minutes. Give a donated prize away to the winning performers, who are chosen by staff members or members of the community serving as judges. This is most often held as a teen program.

Host a singalong. Host a movie night with a twist at your library! Movies with great music like *Frozen*, *Wizard of Oz*, *Grease*, or *Moana* are perfect for singalongs, and you could include some interactive aspects like clicking your heels together whenever Dorothy says the word "home," or tossing around a "snowball" whenever Elsa uses her powers. Be sure you advertise to teens and adults for movies like *Grease*, *Rocky Horror Picture Show*, and *Pitch Perfect*—they are definitely not kid-appropriate!

IDEAS IN ACTION

Stuffed Animal Sleepover

LORI JUHLIN, Hawarden Public Library, Hawarden, Iowa

Stuffed animal sleepovers can be a fun event for kids to see what their furry friends get up to during a night spent in the library. On the Friday afternoon before our first stuffed animal sleepover, children had the opportunity to drop off their stuffed animals at the library and fill out permission forms with contact information. During the sleepover that night, we took pictures of the animals having fun in the library, hearing a story, and we even had a shot of a scared little bunny leaving a trail of Cocoa Puffs after hearing a scary bedtime story! Throughout the evening, we sent texts to the parents to share with their kids.

We host our regular cartoon program on the first Saturday of each month and encourage children to come in their pajamas. We show cartoons and serve cereal and donuts. On that morning, the children could pick up their stuffed animal, and then attend our cartoons program with their animal. But first the children had to find their animal upon arrival at the library, which led to some laughs from kids and parents alike. By tying the two programs together, we increased attendance and made for a fun weekend for the kids.

UPCYCLING PROGRAM IDEAS

Recyclable materials have endless possibilities when it comes to programming, and they are usually very easy to find and collect. Reach out to your community for donations of paper, cardboard, bottles, boxes, whatever you need—they'll often be eager to get rid of them. The following ideas make great use of upcycling materials.

Steal These Ideas!

Create life-size board games. Giant board games are typically easy and cheap to make, and they often use recyclables like cardboard or paper: giant Lego bricks, Minecraft blocks, and huge Angry Bird towers can all be made out of cardboard boxes. You can make a giant Jenga tower by wrapping up empty cardboard 24-packs of soda cans in paper, and then stacking them high. Create a huge Memory game with large pieces of cardstock laid out in a grid. Games like Scrabble, chess, and checkers can be made pretty easily out of thick paper or cardboard, and you can make a giant Twister game outside on the grass with spray paint. Pick-up sticks can be made with some large wooden dowels and paint, and many libraries have come up with a larger-than-life Candyland game, which is typically made using colorful paper and a giant cardboard dice.

FIGURE 2.2

Life-size Jenga with cardboard boxes

Host a drive-in movie night. If you find yourself with an excess of large cardboard boxes, have a drive-in movie night at your library. Have kids decorate the boxes like they're cars, using paper plates for wheels, headlights, and steering wheel, and then hop in to enjoy a drive-in movie. Add some popcorn for a more authentic experience!

Create smash books. An idea for tweens and teens that uses recycled books, magazines, and craft supplies is to make a smash book. A smash book is kind of like a scrapbook, but it doesn't have to include photos—in fact, they are sometimes referred to as "un-scrapbooks." The less formal, organized, and neat you are when creating a smash book, the better—the book is meant to look messy and to reflect how you feel at the moment. A smash book can have a theme (favorite things, a specific band, etc.), but it's more often treated like a journal. Your teens can add in clippings from magazines, bits of ribbon, even googly eyes. It's meant to be a fun, slapdash way of getting your feelings out onto the page. You should provide colorful markers and popular music in the background, and then just let the tweens do their thing

Craft with discarded books. Upcycled book crafts are always a hit with adult patrons. Whether it's making "book pumpkins" or "book flowers," creating bookmarks or origami, or making unique cards to give to their loved ones, these crafts are simple and cheap. And when you include things like buttons, ribbon, twine, and sequins, the possibilities are endless.

IDEAS IN ACTION

Harry Potter Party

CHELSEA PRICE, Meservey Public Library, Meservey, Iowa

My library did a simple, low-cost Harry Potter program that was focused on the tween age group. I created a photo booth using a large piece of recycled cardboard and had the middle schoolers pose as prisoners in Azkaban. They also had "potions class"—making various kinds of slime with some ingredients I had handy at the library or at my own home. For a month or so before the program, I saved up some chopsticks from Chinese restaurants and asked friends to do the same—the attendees used hot glue to make designs on them and then painted them when they dried, and they looked just like the wands from the movies! The kids also watched a *Fantastic Beasts* movie and taste-tested some Bertie Bott's Every Flavor Beans. The jelly beans were the only thing I had to actually purchase for this program, and I found them for a reasonable price on Amazon. The attendees' favorite part of the program was definitely the jelly beans—they included flavors like grass, pepper, and earwax!

11 Hot Money-Saving Tips

1. **Ask for discounts.** You will never know if someone is willing to give you a deal unless you ask.

2. **Use your tax exemption.** If you forget to bring your card on a shopping trip, turn back and come back later when you have the card.

3. **Use volunteers whenever you can.** It is a huge help to have a reliable team of volunteers to help supervise programs, make snacks, or even fill in when a staff member is ill.

4. *DIY whatever you can.* Why spend money when you can make your own whiteboard, flannelboard, magnet board, and storytime props?

5. **Look for a deal.** Dollar stores are a godsend, and you can often find things like Legos or Magnatiles at thrift shops and garage sales.

6. **Check Facebook.** There will often be a community "for sale" or "free" page where you can barter deals on items with people in your neighborhood.

7. **Take surveys.** Check out sites like Swagbucks, Survey Junkie, or Recyclebank, where you can take surveys and thereby earn points to get gift cards and magazine subscriptions.

8. **Use apps to save money.** Using apps like Retail Me Not, Target Circle, Honey, Rakuten, or Ibotta can help you save lots of cash.

9. **Use what you've got.** One of the easiest ways to create a cheap and easy program is to use things you already have, whether it's an abundance of felt or cardboard boxes.

10. **Start a library wish list.** Start a "library wish list" on your library's Amazon page, and include it on your website or Facebook page.

11. **Omit the craft or prize.** Remember that it's okay not to always have a craft, and it's okay to not give away prizes!

Don't Reinvent the Wheel

Librarians can have such high standards for themselves when it comes to programming—"there must always be a craft and a snack!"—and this is just not always realistic. The truth is, if you don't feel like doing a craft and you don't have any supplies handy at the moment . . . it's okay not to do one. Play a game instead, and the kids won't even notice. As far as prizes go, lots of libraries have done away with "cheap plastic junk." Instead, prizes can be things like movie passes, gift cards to local businesses, weeded books and DVDs, candy or food, or "experiences." Experience prizes can include the winner getting a private movie night at the library with three friends, the winner getting to help plan a program or come up with a theme for the next program, or a game night for the winner. Your young patrons will be just as excited, even if they don't have something brightly colored and plastic to take home with them. (Let's be honest, that stuff usually breaks within ten minutes anyway!)

3

Celebrate the Seasons at the Library

IN MANY PARTS OF THE COUNTRY, THE PROGRAMS THAT LIBRARIES offer change depending on the season. As the weather cools and snow threatens, you can't do the outdoor pool noodle sprinkler party anymore. (Well, you could. But you probably don't want to.) And that hot chocolate-making class just doesn't make much sense in the middle of a steaming-hot July.

Holidays of any kind can be stressful for a lot of people—there can be a lot of money, time, and chaos involved. But don't worry: the following easy, low-cost ideas will take the pressure off you and your budget. These inexpensive programming ideas were created with a specific time of year in mind, and they can be done in any library, regardless of its size or budget.

SPRING PROGRAM IDEAS

When the weather warms up, it's time to get outside for your programming. You want to take advantage of the sunshine as soon as you can, especially if you're in an area where winter seems to drag on forever. These ideas are sure to help combat your spring fever!

Steal These Ideas!

Walk it out. Start a walking club, a walking *book* club (walk and talk about what you've been reading), or a dog-walking club. Do an outdoor nature walk or scavenger hunt with your young patrons.

Host an outdoor movie night. Have a movie in the park—a white sheet and a $60 projector from Amazon will work just fine. You don't have to get fancy; everyone loves enjoying a movie outside!

Enjoy a community picnic. Host a community potluck—ask attendees to bring a dish to share, spread blankets out in the park, and enjoy! You could also do a teddy bear picnic in the park as a youth program.

Shoot some springtime photos. You can do a smartphone photography class at any time of year, but it's best to do it outdoors so you can get the best lighting. Take thirty minutes snapping pics outside and then meet back in the library to edit the photos, using free phone apps and YouTube tutorials.

Host an Earth Day or The Lorax program. There are so many crafts which can be created using recycled materials that choosing between them can be almost overwhelming. Making tote bags out of old T-shirts, bird feeders out of milk jugs . . . the list goes on. It can be difficult to narrow the choices down. Consider limiting your Earth Day programs to one specific focus, whether that's planting trees or flowers, feeding the birds, or reusing paper and cardboard. You could empty out your recycle bin and have your young patrons create art from the things they find inside, or just take a nature walk to take in your surroundings and maybe do a few tree bark or leaf rubbings. Include some pudding "dirt cups" for a snack, and you've got yourself a program!

Start a junior gardeners program. Invite a few adult volunteers who are plant-savvy to supervise a group of younger patrons as they plant flowers around your building to beautify the library as spring rolls around!

Offer a stressless program. As spring and the school year draw to a close, high school and college students are often faced with a lot of stress: finals! Ease their pain with a "stressless" program—see if you have any patrons with certified therapy dogs to bring in, and let the frazzled students cuddle with a furry friend. Coloring sheets can also be a huge stress reliever, and you can find a bunch of beautiful designs online. Put out some board games for students to play as they wish, and have a stress ball craft out for them to make. Sometimes just taking a break from studying and having a quiet moment to act like a kid can be a huge help to stressed-out teens.

IDEAS IN ACTION

Project Prom

Kelly Staten, Johnson County Public Library, Franklin, Indiana

https://programminglibrarian.org/programs/project-prom

Project Prom collects gently used prom dresses, tuxedos, shoes, and accessories and gives them to young people in need of formalwear. We started in 2012 and have grown like crazy. This year we had over 300 people attend!

We start planning about six months ahead of time. We hold the program at two library branch locations for three days each. Over time, we have worked with various partners. Local consignment shops have served as donation points for dresses to be dropped off. For several years, a local seamstress even donated her time and expertise to make custom dresses for girls who couldn't find something from the donations.

SUMMER PROGRAM IDEAS

If it's hot, hot, hot outside, don't worry. The following programs will show you how to incorporate some water-themed programming and enjoy the sun.

Steal These Ideas!

Create sun prints. Sun prints are fun for all ages—you can purchase Sun Print Paper at a reasonable price on Amazon. Find uniquely shaped twigs, leaves, and other objects and place them on top of your paper. Leave it outside in a sunny area, and you'll see your paper begin to change in only about five minutes. Rinse the paper under water, and you'll see the prints develop into a frame-worthy piece!

Chalk the walks. Sidewalk chalk is something that most libraries have just lying around. Let your young patrons head outside with it on a warm afternoon and get to work on chalking up the library's sidewalks. Give them a specific thing to draw, or just leave it up to their imagination. Not only is this a free and fun program, but you'll end up with gorgeous, colorful sidewalks!

Host field day. Remember when you were in elementary school, and the last day of school was spent playing games and doing relay races outside? Some schools call it "field day." I always looked forward to that as a kid, and it would be a fun afternoon for libraries to replicate. Try games like a water balloon toss, an egg on the spoon race, a sponge bucket relay race, and a potato sack race. If it's an especially hot day, you could include more water games, like water balloon/water ball slingshots and water gun "painting." Kids tend to love anything involving water, but make sure you let parents know ahead of time that their kids will be coming home drenched in water!

IDEAS IN ACTION

Outdoor Water Party

Jenn Carson, L. P. Fisher Public Library,
Woodstock, New Brunswick, Canada

https://programminglibrarian.org/blog/outdoor-water-party

At the height of your summer reading club or during an autumn back-to-school heat wave, sometimes the best thing to do is to take the kids outside and hose them down—that will get the fidgets out of them! (Just kidding.)

Here are the descriptions of the games:

Duck duck goose. This is played like a regular game of duck duck goose, but the person who is "it" has to break a water balloon over the head of whomever they choose to be the goose.

Sponge bucket relay race. Participants are divided into two even teams and line up on one side of the space. They take turns racing to a bucket filled with water, fill their sponge, and then deposit the water by wringing out the sponge into an empty bucket at the front of their team's line. The first team to transfer enough water—either to float the object or reach the high-water line—wins.

Water balloon toss. In pairs, participants stand across from each other, starting very close together. They pass a water balloon back and forth between them without the balloon breaking. After each toss, participants each take a step away from each other and then toss again. If they break their balloon, they have to return to their starting distance.

Water gun painting. Using cheap water guns from a dollar store, each participant helps paint a piece of art for the library to display. Each kid takes turns shooting at the canvas with their chosen paint color. The kids can switch canvases so they can help paint both. Canvases can also be spun around to mix the colors.

Water fight. This is a free-for-all water balloon fight! This program is a great way to improve physical literacy skills, such as jumping, running, aiming, throwing, carrying, squeezing, and catching, while also improving social skills through teamwork. With all the measuring and counting, we're also improving our math and physics knowledge. We even made some art. The participants loved this event, and they would have stayed all day if we hadn't run out of balloons.

FALL PROGRAM IDEAS

Once the weather cools down and your programs have come back indoors, that means fall and Halloween are right around the corner. Read on for a few autumn ideas.

Steal These Ideas!

Try some pumpkin spice food items. Pumpkin spice lattes are unofficially known as the drink of fall, and it seems like pumpkin spice *everything* has become a real trend in the past few years. There are pumpkin spice drinks, pumpkin spice desserts, pumpkin spice Cheerios, even pumpkin spice popcorn and Oreos! Pick some of these products up at the grocery store, and have them out for attendees of your "Pumpkin Spice Party" to sample. You can even have patrons rate and review the fall-flavored snacks—I'm willing to bet they won't all taste good. As an additional activity, attendees can make a pumpkin spice craft or recipe: there are recipes out there for bath and body products, slime, and no-bake cookies. This event would probably be best for tweens or teens.

Host a Halloween costume exchange. Halloween is tons of fun for young patrons, but sometimes it's more work for parents than we realize. If you see a need for it in your community, consider hosting a costume exchange as a passive program. Collect donations of gently used Halloween costumes throughout the year, and allow parents to browse through your collection. They can take what they need, use it for trick-or-treating, and then return it to the library for someone else to use next year.

IDEAS IN ACTION

Pumpkin Party

CHELSEA PRICE,
Meservey Public Library,
Meservey, Iowa

Each fall, we host a pumpkin party for our young patrons. A generous community member donates around forty pumpkins each year that he grows on his farm. I purchase lots of pumpkin-decorating sticker kits from Oriental Trading at a reasonable price, then

FIGURE 3.1 / Decorated pumpkins

let each attendee grab a pumpkin and start decorating! We also play pumpkin-related games, like pumpkin toss and pumpkin bowling, and we play *It's the Great Pumpkin, Charlie Brown* in the background. It's an inexpensive but beloved program that kids look forward to each year!

WINTER PROGRAM IDEAS

Brrr! The weather is chilly and the holidays are on their way. The following programs are cozy, festive, and sure to be a hit with your community.

Steal These Ideas!

Make your own snow globe. DIY snow globes can be as elaborate or as simple as you'd like. You can use mason jars or, if you adapt the program to be more appropriate for kids, empty baby food jars. Hot-glue little figures to the lid of your jar, add water, glycerin, and glitter, and you've got yourself a snow globe!

Decorate some cookies. Bake some plain sugar cookies (or ask someone to donate them) and purchase or make some colorful frosting. This makes a super-easy holiday program, and the cookies can serve as both your craft and snack!

Host a "Broke Holidays" event. These are basically craft workshops that are used to make cheap or no-cost gifts for loved ones, and they're especially popular with younger adults. Attendees can create things like painted mugs, ornaments, and hot chocolate spoons to give as gifts. This setup would probably be similar to a Pinterest Party—you would put out the supplies and printed-out tutorials, provide some snacks and music, and let your patrons create.

Paint some snow. Depending on your location's winter weather, snow painting is a fun activity for young patrons. Here in the Midwest, you could do snow painting in the months of October all the way through April. All you need are some spray bottles, water, and food coloring or powdered tempera paint (depending on how vibrant you'd like the paint to be). Hand out the bottles and let the kids spray to their hearts' content! Just avoid doing any yellow snow paint. Trust me.

Throw a Noon Year's Eve party. New Year's Eve parties are typically focused solely on adults. And of course, most kids aren't going to make it until midnight to celebrate the New Year (and your library staff won't want to stay up that late anyway). So why not try out a Noon Year's Eve party for your young patrons? A Noon Year's Eve party usually takes place before noon on December 31, and it includes lots of noisemakers, dancing, music, balloons, and a countdown to "midnight." To make your party extra special, include snacks and punch (punch always feels so fancy to kids!), bubbles, and crafts.

IDEAS IN ACTION

Swap Your Stuff: Holiday Style

CHRISTY BILLINGS, Russell Library, Middletown, Connecticut

My library partners with our local recycling department for an event called "Swap Your Stuff." We started with a holiday event last year and have since done a craft swap and an accessories swap to help folks who are in search of a job. The events don't cost anything other than staff time.

This is the event info for our upcoming Holiday Swap:

Swap your Stuff. Holiday Style! Would you like to change out some of your holiday décor, add to your collection, or give away what you can't use anymore? Whichever your circumstances—whether you want to donate your extra holiday decorations and seasonal craft supplies, or acquire some new things—this is the event for you!

Friday, 1:00 pm–5:00 pm. Donations will be accepted. All items must be intact, in good condition, and no larger than two feet square. Only holiday items and seasonal craft supplies will be accepted. No trees, please. Each donor will receive a ticket for admission to Saturday's Early Bird Browsing.

Saturday, 9:00 am–10:00 am. Early Bird Browsing will be open to everyone who donated on Friday.

Saturday, 10:00 am–11:30 am. Everyone is welcome to browse and take anything they can use, whether they donated to the swap on Friday or not.

Hot beverages will be served. Reduce, reuse, recycle! All items remaining at the close of the swap will be donated.

Wrap & Yap

CHELSEA PRICE, Meservey Public Library, Meservey, Iowa

I came up with this idea when I was wrapping my Christmas gifts by myself at home in front of the TV. I was bored and thought to myself, "Wouldn't it be so much more fun to do this with a group of friends and some snacks?" Thus the Wrap & Yap program was born. I have hosted this adult program at my library for three years now, and it has gone well every time. Around twelve adults (which is great for my library—it's tough for us to get a good turnout at adult programs) show up to chitchat, have some snacks, and wrap their holiday gifts.

Each attendee brings their own gifts to wrap, wrapping paper, bows and ribbons, and gift tags to share with the group, and the library provides scissors, tape, and light snacks. I put on a holiday radio station quietly in the background, and everyone has a wonderful time catching up with the group. To make this even more cost-effective, you could have attendees bring snacks to share, making this program completely free!

Christmas Store

LILL BATSON, Viola Public Library District, Viola, Illinois

The Children's Christmas Store was started fourteen years ago when the local school district stopped offering Santa's Closet for children to purchase Christmas gifts. We partner with our Friends group and our Royal Neighbors of America chapter (part of the Royal Neighbors of America charitable foundation). We have partnered with other Royal Neighbor chapters in the area to provide free gift-wrapping for the children. The past few years, we have used volunteers for the gift-wrapping. The store is open for children up to age eighteen.

The first year, we held the store at the library with various tables set up— one with items for men, one with items for women, one for children, a miscellaneous gift table, and a gift-wrapping table. Items were priced from $0.10 to $1.00. The first year we had approximately thirty children attend the store, and we sold out almost everything. We also had Santa and Mrs. Claus here to visit with children and take their Santa letters. We hold the store in the fellowship hall at the Methodist Church, since we have outgrown any other space available in town. We usually have over 100 children from the area who shop for Christmas. Santa and Mrs. Claus have retired, but we still accept Santa letters and write back to the children.

Over the years, our store has grown. To make things easier on everyone, we started charging $1.00 per item. We purchase nice jewelry (usually on clearance), tools, perfume, gloves, socks, ties, puzzles, stuffed animals, baby items, snacks, handmade items—including scarves, hats, mittens, slippers, shawls, and quilted items—toys of all kinds, Pokemon cards—pretty much anything we can find that kids might want.

We get some items donated (mostly handmade items); however, we raise funds all year to pay for the items. Children and their parents look forward to the store each year. Any money made at the store goes into the next year's store. Our Christmas Store is not a moneymaker, just a great chance to give back to the community. Everyone has a great time watching the children choose the gifts they will give. This definitely makes the Christmas season a little better. Our Christmas Store is something we are very proud of.

Holiday Inclusivity

There are many libraries that decorate and program for specific holidays, such as Halloween, Christmas, and Easter. For many patrons, certain holidays represent nostalgia, comfort, and joy, and it can be difficult to leave them out of your programming. However, as libraries, we serve everyone—regardless of their culture or religion. It is important for us to be aware of how these types of programs might affect someone who is not Christian or who doesn't believe in celebrating days like Halloween. Maybe our holiday programming and décor make them feel uncomfortable and unwelcome at the library. We must keep in mind that inclusivity doesn't just mean all people who celebrate Christian holidays. It doesn't just mean the majority, either. It means everyone. It's something I'm working on at my library, and you should be, too. (For more on this, read Kendra Jones's 2014 piece on Storytime Underground titled "Librarians—Check Your Holidays at the Door.")

12 Nontraditional Holidays to Celebrate at Your Library

1. Trivia Day—January 4
2. Galentine's Day—February 13
3. National Puppy Day—March 23
4. Children's Book Day—April 2
5. Star Wars Day—May 4
6. National Selfie Day—June 21
7. Embrace Your Geekness Day—July 13
8. National Tell a Joke Day—August 16
9. Read a Book Day—September 6
10. National Pasta Day—October 17
11. National Author's Day—November 1
12. Letter Writing Day—December 7

4

The Librarian Has Left the Building

OUTREACH—IT'S JUST WHAT IT SOUNDS LIKE: REACHING OUT TO those who may not be aware of what your library has to offer. When you leave that circulation desk to venture out beyond the walls of your library building, your library has no limits! You can go out into your community and sing the praises of all the wonderful services you offer. Sounds simple, right? So why does it so often fall by the wayside in many libraries?

Well, for one thing, outreach can be intimidating. You're out of your "safe space," and things aren't as under your control as they might be during a regular program. Many small libraries believe they simply don't have the manpower to do outreach—they don't have the staff, the budget, or the time. Other libraries just might not know how to get started. Whom do you contact? Where do you go? What do you bring with you? This chapter will help you jump head-first into outreach (if you haven't already), get excited about new places to visit, and learn about best practices when you're out and about.

GETTING STARTED

Find out where your community is. Ask yourself this question, and figure out where people (adults, children, teens, and families) in your community tend to congregate. Is it at a community center? At the park? The swimming pool? Maybe it's at a bar or brewery?

Go there . . . Once you've figured out where the people are, meet them there! Get out of those stacks and into your community. You can tailor your outreach to each location—do a children's storytime at the swimming pool during breaks, bring discarded cookbooks to your table at the farmer's market, offer information on early literacy to parents when you're at kindergarten roundup. Go where the people are rather than waiting for them to come to you. Not only does this give you a chance to meet people where they are at, it also gives you opportunities to get to know your community. You'll eventually get an idea of what their needs are, whether you have gaps in your programs and services, and what might be keeping them from coming in your doors.

. . . *but ask permission!* You probably don't need permission to go to a public space like a park, but you'll definitely want to double-check on most locations when you're doing outreach. Never show up at a location unannounced and just expect to be able to do a quick storytime or set up a table—it's not going to happen. Reach out to someone in charge at least a few weeks beforehand to make your plans. This can be as simple as an e-mail. Here's an example of an e-mail you might send to a day care center:

> Hi there! My name is _____, and I'm the _____ at the _____ Public Library. We are looking to do some more outreach in the community, and I was wondering if you might be interested in letting us visit once a month or so to do a storytime. We bring all of our own materials, so you would not need to provide anything except the children! Our storytimes typically include two or three short books, a fingerplay, some fun and interactive songs, and an activity, easy craft, or flannelboard. The storytimes can also be tailored to fit different age groups. Let me know what you think! I look forward to hearing from you!

Many times when a library contacts an organization or business, it is asking them for something, whether it's a donation, a service, or a favor. So when you contact an organization to offer to do something for *them* and ask nothing in return, many people will be pleasantly surprised. Go anywhere you're welcome, and think outside the box. Once you've become a regular visitor at community events, people will come to expect you there and ask for you—you'll eventually become something of a rock star, especially at children's events!

WHY DO OUTREACH?

Libraries do outreach so that they can offer amazing services to *everyone*, regardless of whether they ever come into the library building or not. Lots of people don't live within walking distance of a library and don't have readily available transportation. You may have a few shut-ins in your community—people who rarely leave their home—who are missing out on the great materials you offer. Some people may be intimidated by walking into a library, recalling memories of stern-faced librarians shushing them. Others may think that libraries are all about books—they might not even be aware that you offer tons of online resources, free programs, and fun events. To be quite honest, there are probably quite a few people who don't even know that a library exists in their community. Outreach helps you get to those people.

It's all about community engagement—meeting people where they're comfortable in order to offer services and promote the library. Making non-users aware of your offerings is an essential part of what you do as a librarian. A quote from a *Library Journal* article sums it up nicely: "The services the library offers are as important for those who don't walk into the library as for those who do."

An added benefit of outreach is that you can form some amazing connections. Working in a small library means that much of your job is basically defined by relationships—with your patrons, city council, community, donors, local business owners, and so on. By visiting a business you've never been to before and pulling off an awesome storytime or setting up a popular table, the owner will probably be interested in continuing a working relationship with your library, and this could lead to some great partnership opportunities in the future. When you're outside the library, you never know who you might meet that's interested in helping you out.

In many cases, outreach can count in your program numbers. When you report to your city, county, or state, they'll see those increased program numbers and be impressed. If you start a bookmobile, and lend books out to schools, day care centers, or individuals, your circulation numbers can increase dramatically. Plus, it's just good PR for your library; it really makes an impact on your community members to see you—the "face" of the library—outside the building doing fun things to spread the word about your services.

WHERE TO GO?

School outreach might seem obvious (we'll talk about that in another chapter), but where else can you go? Places with a built-in audience are especially good opportunities for outreach—there will be people there no matter what, so why not entertain them for a few minutes? What about a themed storytime at a nature center, or a storytime with preschoolers at a local senior center? Or bringing books and information on early literacy to a birthing center or a pediatrician's waiting room? You could offer tech help with phones or tablets at senior centers, or try out a dog- and cat-themed storytime at a local animal shelter. Some libraries are creating pop-up libraries in local laundromats, bringing reading materials and learning tools for families to enjoy while they're waiting on their laundry. One library took the "Blind Date with a Book" idea out into their community, venturing out with a bunch of wrapped-up, discarded books and some chocolate and handing them out to whoever seemed interested.

Steal These Ideas!

Visit a comic-con. Set up a table at a local comic-con event, and include a geeky craft and information about upcoming programs that may be of interest. Bring Bingo cards that people can take around to different booths and vendors to get a signature or stamp, and give away a prize to those who return a full card. Bonus points if you dress in costume!

Read stories at a domestic violence shelter. Consider doing an outreach story-time at a domestic violence shelter or similar organization. Prepare the story-time to be appropriate for several different age groups rather than just aiming it at infants or toddlers. Bring sensory toys and a simple craft, and if there are older children present, try to enlist them as helpers. Prior to the storytime, you could collect toy donations from your community and give them out to attendees of the storytime (with permission from the organization).

Hang out at an art festival. Outdoor festivals of any kind are full of opportunities for outreach. Set up a table displaying art-themed books, and have a craft out for children to create their very own art projects.

Share information with a mom group. If there is a local parent group that meets regularly in your area, get permission to stop by with parenting books and learning materials to share, and make sure to talk up your children's collection as well.

Visit a health expo. It's always great when libraries promote health and wellness, and a health expo or fair is an easy way to get involved. Display your favorite health-related books, cookbooks, DVDs, and magazines, and for bonus points, offer a healthy snack to passersby! You could do the same type of outreach at your local yoga studio, gym, or YMCA.

Share stories at the zoo. Your local zoo may have visited your library, but I bet your library has yet to visit *them*! Doing a storytime at the zoo (or aquarium, or petting zoo) is a fun twist on traditional programming—be sure to bring some animal-related props!

Partner up with a correctional facility. Most correctional facilities don't have a large book selection; work with your local jail or juvenile detention facility to make sure there are some great books available for those who need them.

Read stories at the park. There's nothing like an outdoor storytime! Choose a sunny afternoon and have a pop-up storytime at your local park, beach, swimming pool, wherever.

Visit a laundromat. Laundromat libraries have been in the news quite a bit lately, and for good reason. There's a lot of waiting going on at laundromats, so why not provide an opportunity for families to read and learn together while they wait? This strategy of providing literacy in ordinary locations can do wonders, particularly in areas that are considered "book deserts."

TIPS FOR WHEN YOU'RE OUT AND ABOUT

Don't reinvent the wheel. It's okay to do the same storytime for every classroom or day care center you visit. Don't make things harder for yourself by trying to come up with something new, exciting, and different every single time. Sometimes a folding table and chair, an eye-catching sign, and handouts about upcoming library programs are all you'll need at outreach events—don't feel as though you always need a bunch of razzle-dazzle.

Bring fun extras. Speaking of razzle-dazzle, there will be other times when you'll want to hand out swag, bring a craft, and play a game—and that's fine too. Having visual displays is always a good idea. Kids and teens will be more likely to respond to you if you have a few extra goodies to draw them in. This could be a prize wheel for them to spin, an "I Spy" poster that they can look at to hunt down specific pictures, or even a mobile makerspace like a button maker, crafts, or coloring sheets. For adult events, consider bringing along a few discarded books and DVDs, and see if anyone is willing to give a free-will donation to purchase some. As far as swag goes, color-changing pencils and scratch-and-sniff bookmarks are always a hit. Oh, and bring tape—*always* bring tape. You'll end up needing it for one thing or another. Just trust me on this one.

Be flexible. Outreach events are very different from events held inside the library. Many things will be outside of your control, and this idea of "entering into the unknown" can be unsettling to some. It's important to be flexible and adaptable when you're doing outreach, and remember that just because you have certain expectations for the event doesn't mean that that's what will end up happening. You can plan and plan and plan, but things can still go awry. Have a backup plan in case of weather, an unexpected school cancellation, or if the public simply doesn't respond well to your event.

Have fun! Dance around, sing a song, make a complete fool out of yourself! Don't be afraid to be silly, particularly if you're doing a children's event. People pick up on whether or not you're having a good time at outreach events, and if they can tell that you are, they will have a good time too. Many librarians (myself included) are introverts, but try as hard as you can to force out that extrovert you have inside! Get out from behind the table, greet people, and make eye contact! Sometimes that can make all the difference. You might feel incredibly out of your element at first, but once you start making the initial move to talk to people, you will quickly grow more comfortable. Your goal is to get people excited about your library, and the way to reach that goal is by being approachable and enthusiastic.

IDEAS IN ACTION

Mobile Planetarium Outreach

BETH ANDERSON, Clarksburg-Harrison Public Library,
Clarksburg, West Virginia

We partnered with our local Moose Lodge and did a Bingo fundraiser that provided the funding for us to bring a mobile planetarium in. (This is an inflatable plastic dome, and a simulation of the night sky is projected onto its interior.) We also partnered with the local elementary school for the location, as the planetarium was very large. Throughout the day, each class attended a special presentation in the planetarium picked for them by library staff, in consultation with school faculty. Then after school, we were able to have four presentations that were open to the public. This was part of a series of space-related programs that our intern planned as a part of his Summer of Space/Solar Eclipse Program.

Pumpkin Patch Storytime

CHELSEA PRICE, Meservey Public Library, Meservey, Iowa

Once a year, I do a fall storytime at a local pumpkin patch. I bring along some fall-themed books and an easy craft (usually ordered from Oriental Trading). We sit in the barn along a circular rug, and afterward, the kids have s'mores (provided by the pumpkin patch owner). When I came on board as director, our library had never done outreach before—not even school visits. So it was interesting to come up with different ideas on my own. It's great to get to offer a storytime to a bunch of new faces . . . and sometimes those faces show up later at an in-house program, which is so rewarding!

Storytime Swim

KIM KIETZMAN and SHEILA OLSON,
Altoona Public Library, Altoona, Iowa

We have hosted Storytime Swim for the last five years. It was set up by the previous children's librarian by partnering with the Altoona Campus, a nonprofit recreational center in the area. The plan was to have an outdoor storytime that would be free and open to the public. The campus agreed to allow free admission to families during the event.

The Altoona Campus Aquatic Center now hosts Storytime Swim every Wednesday in June and July after morning swim lessons and before they open to the public. Two or three lifeguards are on duty during that time, and the attendees stay in the shallow end of the pool. The water slides and fountains are turned off, but the locker rooms are open. I stand by the door to count people and greet them as they enter, making sure they know the rules of Storytime Swim.

I use a lapel mic and a portable speaker so I can be heard over the crowd while I read the storytimes. I usually bring two books that are highly interactive to keep the kids involved and moving in the pool. I also do three songs that I play over the speaker. I try to keep these highly interactive and energetic as well. At the end, I bounce beach balls into the crowd, and the families have about ten minutes to swim and play together before we start asking them to get out of the pool.

This program is something that families ask about each year. It has been amazing to see it grow, and it has been a great way to show new families what Altoona has to offer. The campus has had many participants join after seeing the pool during the storytime. This past year, they had to add another lifeguard because our group was so large. The record attendance, counting children and guardians, is 226 people. It is talked about all year long and is a definite favorite of Altoona families.

The success of Storytime Swim has encouraged us to find other businesses to partner with in the community. We now do storytimes at the local ice cream shop and are in talks to have a storytime at the supermarket. We also reach out to community members to visit our library, such as police officers, dentists, musicians, and other community helpers, and be guests at our weekly storytimes. All of these programs are free and are promoting community unity. We have found that the more you talk to people and ask, the more opportunities present themselves.

Prizeless Prize Wheel

S. BRYCE KOZLA

https://brycekozlablog.blogspot.com/

My favorite outreach tool is our library's prize wheel (a round wheel that you can spin to determine what you will win). It was purchased from Amazon for around $45, and it has a dry-erase surface for you to write in the prizes (or, in our case, actions). A coworker and I took the wheel to a health fair on behalf of our cooperative. This was a "tabling event," as opposed to an outreach event like a class visit. I have a hard-held belief that at events like this, the library can have the most popular table on the block. And at the health fair, we did!

For our "swag," we brought color-changing pencils left over from our summer reading program (they are worth every cent!) and stickers promoting our 1,000 Books before Kindergarten program. But what really made a difference and drew people to our table was our prize wheel. We had people flocking to our table to see what the fuss was about, laughing with each other, and taking pictures.

Here's what I think made it so successful:

The wheel was the whole point. The goal wasn't to spin the wheel to win a prize. The kids walked away with a pencil no matter what, so there was nothing that could only be won by spinning the wheel, and no one was disappointed because due to luck they ended up with something they didn't want.

The wheel was full of actions. Rather than telling you what you've won, the wheel determined whether you "had to" name a nearby library, tell us a good book you've read or movie you've seen, or play air guitar and say, "I love my library!" People could always spin again if they wanted to do something different, and they could spin multiple times if it wasn't too busy.

We were ready to play. We embraced the silliness to really take our wheel participation to the next level. We were both out from behind the table, doing the actions with everyone and calling out, "I love my library!" because that was the part which many people forgot at first. Doing the actions *with* our visitors helped them be less shy about doing them themselves. At one point, we had ten people from three different families gathered around the wheel to see what action they could get and do all together. And at that moment I knew we'd made it.

Here are the questions I used: name a nearby library, name one thing you can get with a library card, tell us a good movie or show you've seen, and tell us a good book you've read. And here are the actions I used, all including calling out "I love my library!": dance like a robot, make a silly face, play air guitar, jump up and down, and pose like a superhero.

Book Yak on a Kayak

CHRISTY BILLINGS, Russell Library, Middletown, Connecticut

The idea for the kayak program came from our doing book discussions in unique ways. The previous summer, we had started "Book Talk with a Walk." We would meet at the library and walk along the Connecticut River, stopping in three locations to discuss books which had been previous community reads.

In 2019, we partnered with our local Parks and Recreation Department to get our patrons out on Crystal Lake to discuss *The River* by Peter Heller. We asked that people who needed a kayak or canoe reserve one by e-mail, and we required registration from all participants.

The Parks and Recreation Department had two canoes and two kayaks, and our library staff had two extra kayaks. Some of our participants had kayaks but no practical way to transport them, but they brought their personal flotation devices and their paddles. Parks and Recreation had a waiver for participants to sign, as well as flotation devices for everyone who needed one.

I had book discussion cards that we created for the outdoor book discussions and for our Books and Brews and Yoga book discussions. In this case, the cards were laminated, but no one lost their questions to the water.

We had eleven participants for our inaugural event. The only cost involved was staff time; none of the book discussions have any costs associated with them beyond my time. A few lessons I learned: have a second staff member who can help with the waivers, and hand out the questions before leaving the dock. The community has responded that they would like more discussions on the water!

This was the PR for our program. "Russell Library and the Middletown Park and Rec are partnering for a one-of-a-kind book discussion. Meet us at Crystal Lake in Middletown to discuss *The River* by Peter Heller aboard kayaks or canoe. Registration is required for all paddlers. Participants may bring their own paddle craft/personal flotation device, or borrow a PFD.

"A limited number of kayaks/canoes are available. To reserve one, please e-mail us. Please arrive by 9:45 a.m. We will leave the dock promptly at 10:00 a.m. Rain cancels the event. A big thank you to the Middletown Park and Rec, for partnering with us for this unique book discussion." The program was also featured in our Connecticut Libraries Association newsletter.

GO FORTH AND OUTREACH!

Do you feel prepared yet? Are you ready to get out there and do some outreach? If you're still worried about not having the time, money, or staff, just remember that you don't have to do outreach events every week, or even every month. As long as you're doing a few quality events consistently throughout the year, that's plenty. Quality really is more important than quantity in this case.

You can also try reaching out to volunteers. If you honestly feel like you'll collapse if you try to fit just one more thing into your schedule, see if someone else can help. Either they can man the library for an hour or two while you do a quick school visit, or you can train them to do outreach events on their own. Just remember that whoever you send out into the community will be representing your library, so choose wisely!

Keep your mind open, and try anything once. If you don't like a specific location or event, guess what? You never have to go back. If you don't enjoy an outreach event or you don't feel it was beneficial to the community, put an end to it. You don't need to say yes to everything or spread yourself too thin.

Outreach can sometimes be undervalued by trustees, boards, and city councils. Maybe they don't think you're reaching enough people, or that it's a waste of library time. Maybe they aren't seeing circulation or attendance numbers increase as a result of your outreach efforts, and they don't think it's doing anything to improve the library or community. With tight budgets and an already-harried staff, outreach can be a hard sell. This needs to change!

Outreach is not about the numbers. It's not about getting a high door count or bringing people in droves to your in-house programs. It's about outcomes and, again, quality over quantity. It doesn't matter *how many* people you're reaching, it's just that you're reaching them! You're making a difference in the community simply by offering these services outside of your building, and that is a worthwhile and commendable effort

5

There's Gold in Them Thar Hills!

DID YOU KNOW THAT YOUR COMMUNITY—YES, YOURS!—IS CHOCK-full of shining pieces of gold? It's true! The mayor, the fire chief, the school band teacher . . . the dental hygienist, the high school quarterback, the local bar owner . . . All of these people represent gleaming pieces of programming gold! The potential for amazing library programs is inside of everyone, and it's up to you to mine that gold and create those relationships, connections, and partnerships.

Partnerships should be the cornerstone of a small library's programming plans. They make things easier on you and your staff, they are often very cheap or even free, and they increase the library's visibility and allow you to draw in some new patrons. These days, libraries are constantly having their budgets cut, and we keep having to find new and innovative ways to make the most of our funding—and for this reason, collaborations are an incredibly resourceful and savvy option. In this chapter, we're going to talk all about partnerships and how you can put on successful, low-cost or free programs at your library by teaming up with the many people who make up your community. There are so many possibilities for partnership right at your fingertips, and you may not even be aware of them!

10 Benefits of Partnerships

1. Quality programming for minimal expense

2. Raise the visibility of the library

3. Gain more advocates for your library

4. Reach an audience you may not have reached otherwise, in turn reinvigorating circulation and program attendance

5. Offer a wider variety of programs

6. Funders like seeing these partnerships, and it may result in more funding for the library

7. Increase the level and quality of programming

8. Increase grant opportunities

9. Create community connections

10. Increase staff satisfaction through learning new things and nurturing new relationships

GETTING STARTED

Tour your own community. Before you start asking around for programming collaborations, make sure you know what is going on in your community first. Get out of the library and explore your town and surrounding towns. Take note of what businesses there are—both chains and local mom-and-pop stores—as well as what other libraries or community centers have going on. This can help you get an idea of what the community needs and what it doesn't. For example, if a church or other nearby organization has a family craft night on Thursday evenings, you should probably avoid doing a craft program of your own on Thursdays. If you only spend time inside your library and don't take the time to explore your town, you could be missing out on all sorts of possibilities.

Introduce yourself. Once you're aware of your surroundings, pop into some of those stores and businesses (make sure it's at a time when business is slow) and introduce yourself to the owners. Keep it brief and polite—simply tell them your name, what library you work at, and explain that you're trying to familiarize yourself with local places and get to know your community a bit better. Don't ask them for anything during your first visit; just let them know that you are a phone call away if they ever need anything. Learn their names and commit them to memory.

Ask questions of your community. Consider sending out a survey to your community. Ask them not only what they'd like to see from their local library, but also what they'd like from their community in general. What is lacking in the community? What do they enjoy about what's offered locally? If surveys don't work well in your town, you can also ask patrons in person as they come in, or non-patrons you run into at the post office or the bank. Most people will be open to having a two-minute conversation about how to improve their community. Find out what really matters to the people of your town so you can work toward making it happen.

Keep it simple. When you have introduced yourself to the business owner, organization leader, or community member you have in mind for a future collaboration and you've had a few interactions with them unrelated to programming, you're ready to ask them if they'd be interested in partnering up. Keep it simple the first time you ask: it's as easy as a single question: "Would you ever be interested in doing a short presentation on _____ at the library?" or "Is there a chance you might be willing to donate _____ for our summer reading program?" Act enthusiastic and excited about whatever you're asking, and explain what the library could do for them in return, whether that's paying them to present or having their business cards available at the circulation desk. If they say yes, great—you've just formed your first partnership! If they say no, don't worry—you've planted the seed of something in their head, and there's always a chance they'll change their mind in the future.

CONNECT WITH LOCAL BUSINESSES

Checking out your town's local small businesses is a great place to start. Mom-and-pop shops and restaurants are often happy to help out their town library because they know that doing so might drum up some new business for themselves. Just remember that one good turn deserves another—if a business has helped your library out in any way, be sure to spread the word by leaving positive reviews on their social media pages, referring patrons to them, and putting out their business cards at the events they help out at. In small towns, it's so important for small businesses (and nonprofits) to help one another out.

Steal These Ideas!

Host a spa night or makeup tutorial program. Invite a local hairdresser or makeup artist to help program attendees get glam.

Hold a flower-arranging class. Ask a local florist if they would be willing to teach patrons how to create a beautiful arrangement.

Host a senior-centric computer course. Is there a computer tech business in town or a local "IT guy"? See if they might be interested in teaching your town's seniors how to do things like set up an e-mail address, navigate the internet, or FaceTime their relatives.

Host a cupcake-decorating class. Contact a local bakery and invite them to teach a cake- or cookie-decorating course at your library. They also might be willing to donate snacks to future youth programs.

Get your yoga on. Ask around at local yoga studios or gyms that might like to come teach a brief beginner's yoga class at the library, in order to advertise and give patrons an idea of what regular classes would be like.

IDEAS IN ACTION

Floral Pumpkin Workshop

CHELSEA PRICE, Meservey Public Library, Meservey, Iowa

Our town has a very popular florist, a one-woman show who has been making arrangements for local weddings, funerals, and parties for years. She also happens to be very crafty! I contacted her near Halloween one year and asked if she might be willing to partner up with the library to do something involving . . . pumpkins. She was excited and immediately came up with the idea of making floral pumpkins—miniature pumpkins hollowed out, with a small votive holder inside full of beautiful autumn-colored flowers. She also brought some decorations to include on the pumpkins, like spiders and skulls. We had

FIGURE 5.1 / Floral pumpkin workshop

fifteen adults, and they had so much fun—I couldn't believe their creativity! When I offered to pay the florist for her time or reimburse her for the flowers, she refused, so the only thing the library ended up paying for were twenty votive holders from the Dollar Tree store! The workshop got great feedback, and patrons have requested that she hold another class near the holidays.

Photos with Santa

CHELSEA PRICE, Meservey Public Library, Meservey, Iowa

Prior to the Photos with Santa program, I had tried to do a couple of winter storytimes and a showing of the movie *The Polar Express* . . . but only two kids showed up. I saw the popularity of local events that offered pictures with Santa, and decided to, yes, steal that idea! I borrowed a Santa suit from our city hall—they use it each year at their holiday prize drawing—and I was (barely) able to talk (bribe) my husband into being Santa for the day. I also contacted a local photographer who had a fairly new business, and I asked her if she might be interested in partnering up. Not only was she interested, she was thrilled to be included! She refused any pay, and only asked that she could give parents her business card.

I purchased some ice cream cones, green frosting, and small candies, and I also bought some red and silver fabric to use as a photo backdrop. Those were the only costs to the library. The attendees made miniature "Christmas trees" by frosting the upside-down ice cream cones and decorating them with candy; these served as both a craft *and* a snack. Then Santa (who may or may not have been hiding in a closet) came out to pose for some photos with the kids, and the kids were thrilled. The photographer snapped some great pictures, and the parents were very pleased when she said she would send them for free in an e-mail. This was a successful holiday program that cost next to nothing, and the photographer ended up getting some future business out of it!

Back-to-School Pizza Party

CHELSEA PRICE, Meservey Public Library, Meservey, Iowa

Each year, a local bank gives the library a small grant of $250 to purchase backpacks and school supplies for kids who need them. Casey's General Store also donates a couple of large pizzas, and the library purchases drinks and a few craft supplies. Kids of all ages flock to free pizza (or food of any kind, really), and they stay to decorate notebooks and make some cool decorations for their lockers. At the end of the program, we give the backpacks away—we usually ask on Facebook and in person if patrons would like to enter their child to win, and then we draw names. The kids and parents are always overjoyed to win free stuff, and everyone goes home happy!

ENLIST THE PEOPLE YOU KNOW

You can also "partner up" with individuals you know, whether it's to share their talents through a program or just showcase their amazing geode collection at your library. I'm willing to bet that just about everyone you know has a hidden talent, interest, skill, or collection, and some of them just might be persuaded to share it with an audience for a library program. After all, why shell out big bucks for a pricey performer when your father-in-law is an expert storyteller, or your old friend from college teaches children's yoga at the local YMCA?

If you want to brainstorm ideas for programs, start making a list of the people you know—family members, friends, acquaintances, coworkers—who have interesting hobbies, jobs, talents, and so on. (You could also go through your Facebook friend list.) Try to really think outside the box when you make the list; you can create a program out of just about anything. Gardening, bee-keeping, raising chickens, grooming dogs, building computers, painting, cooking, dramatic reading—these could all make for successful programs!

Think about if someone is in a club, choir, organization, or volunteer group. Are they on the chamber of commerce, in the parks and recreation department, the local historical society? Make note if they have an interesting pet, have gone on a unique and amazing trip, or play an instrument. Whether they take flawless photos on Instagram with the perfect filters, have a passion for animal rescue, or are very into their comic book collection . . . there's a program there. Everyone is good at something; it's just a matter of finding out what their talent or passion is and nurturing it. As you can see, the possibilities are endless, and so many programs could be right there under your nose!

When your list is done, it's time to go down the list and weed out the ideas that you know won't work at this time. Don't toss them out completely—just set them aside for a later date. If you know that someone has a lot on their plate right now and you don't feel comfortable asking, take them off your list. If you find out that the policies at your library won't allow animal visits, take those off your list. If the city won't allow you to serve alcohol at the library, take the wine tasting/brewery idea off your list. You might not feel comfortable having a program dealing with religion or politics at your library—take those off your list.

Depending on your relationship with the individual, decide whether you're going to call, e-mail, text, or ask in person. It's important to make separate requests to each person—don't just send out one mass e-mail; that could feel impersonal and rude. Tailor your message to fit each person. Keep it casual, and start with a compliment. Don't ask for a specific date just yet—you're just testing the waters to see if they would be interested in possibly doing something in the future.

Here's an example of a message you could send:

> Hi there! You probably know that I am the library director at the Anytown Library, and I am always brainstorming different ideas for programs. I have been looking through all of the photos of the special effects makeup you've done this year—you're so talented! I'm not sure if you would ever be interested in doing a program at the library, but our teens would LOVE a special effects makeup class! It could especially be great for a Halloween program. We would be happy to compensate you for your time. Let me know what you think!

This message is low-pressure, complimentary, and simple. You should only include the part about compensating them if it's in your budget. There's a chance that some people would be more than happy to put on a program for free. That example is a message I might send to a Facebook friend or someone I went to school with. You would probably be much less formal with a spouse or a sibling. (You never know: "COME TO MY LIBRARY AND DO A PROGRAM" might actually work!)

Though there might be some people on your list who you think will say no, keep them on the list and reach out anyway. The worst they can say is "no," and you'll never know if you don't try. In a small library, it's important to take chances and make mistakes. And again, even if they turn you down, you've planted the idea in their mind, and that's what matters.

Steal These Ideas!

Hold a video game "petting zoo." Maybe your brother has an awesome collection of old-school video games and gaming systems—why not borrow them and have a video game "petting zoo," allowing your patrons to try out a bunch of nostalgic games?

Work out at the library. Is your mother-in-law a fitness instructor? See if she'd be willing to teach a Zumba class at your library.

Educate your patrons on animal health and safety. Got an old high school pal who is now a veterinarian? Invite him to talk to your patrons about keeping their pets safe and healthy.

Host a storytelling night. Perhaps you have a grandfather who is an army veteran with many amazing stories to tell. Ask him to share those stories with an audience at your library.

Create beautiful wreaths. Let's say you have a neighbor who loves to create all kinds of wreaths that she finds on Pinterest. Invite her to teach her skills in a wreath-making class.

IDEAS IN ACTION

Fun Palace

BEKA LEMONS, Huntington City-Township
Public Library, Huntington, Indiana

In 2017, the Huntington City-Township Public Library became the first library in the United States to hold an officially sanctioned "Fun Palace." Originating in the United Kingdom, Fun Palaces are community events that offer hands-on art and learning in public spaces. The goal is to let people try new things in a free and open event. There is a strong focus on making sure that there are only activities that people can actually touch and try—there are no lectures in a Fun Palace. In the first year, the Huntington Fun Palace attracted over 500 participants in two days, and in the subsequent years we have had 350–500 people. We also routinely have more than 50 staff and community volunteers holding the activities.

At the Huntington Fun Palace, a wide variety of activities have been offered. Painting is always a staple because there are always painting supplies on hand that don't need to be purchased specially for the event. We have done "Paint Like Pollock," tile painting, squirt gun painting, and rock painting with very little extra cost. One of the greatest assets for the Fun Palaces has been our staff. Every year our staffers volunteer their time and materials to provide activities like cross-stitching, calligraphy, scrapbooking, cake-decorating, meditation, stretching, and much more.

Our community has also been very supportive and active. Our local LARPing (live action role-playing) group comes every year to let folks try on their costumes and play with foam weapons, and they have as much fun as our patrons do! A local music store has also participated every year, providing free musical instruments for our Instrument Petting Zoo. We have also had bee-keepers, physical therapists, falconers, dance teachers, 4-H groups, the local tattoo parlor (yes, we did Sharpie tattoos), hula-hoopers, knitters, gamers, and so much more. The city even provided us with a dump truck and fire truck for a "Touch-a-Truck" station.

FIGURE 5.2

Even dogs can get involved in the Fun Palace!

Most of the time and materials are donated, but we do spend some money on supplies and advertising. The one thing that we did spend a bit of money on was getting the local science center to send a staff member and a variety of science activities. All of the money for programs is provided by our Friends of the Library group. Fun Palaces can be big or small, so even if a library can only provide one or two activities for the weekend, that is okay.

Canvas-Painting Program

CHELSEA PRICE, Meservey Public Library, Meservey, Iowa

The canvas-painting program was a very popular program at my library. My high school friend's sister is the owner of a salon in town, and she used to do wine & canvas-painting nights for adults on the side. After a few people asked her if she would ever host a painting night for kids, she contacted me to see if the library wanted to partner up. We did several kids' painting parties, and they were such a hit! She would come to the library with all of the supplies needed—the library just provided a tarp for the floor (gotta protect that carpet!) and some tables. She would then walk them through a simple, fun painting. The kids had a blast, and parents loved seeing their children's finished projects! We reimbursed her for the supplies she purchased specifically for that program (usually just the canvases), which ended up being only a fraction of what we would have paid had we tried to do it ourselves or hire someone to teach the class.

TRACK DOWN HOMETOWN HEROES

Think like a kid: who was your hero when you were young? Besides the obvious answers like a parent, older sibling, or Marvel character, who did you look up to? Perhaps a favorite teacher? The star of the high school basketball team? Make another list, this time of people around town who could be considered local heroes. Try to think about regular people who do extraordinary things—there are many out there!

Here are a few examples:

- Town mayor
- School principal
- Park ranger
- Big Brothers/Big Sisters
- Veterinarian
- Fire chief
- School nurse
- Founder of local food bank
- Doctor/pediatrician
- Cheerleading captain
- Football quarterback
- War veteran
- Teacher
- Paramedic
- Coach
- Local TV or radio personality

Sure, maybe not every one of these examples could create a successful program. But your hometown heroes could read a book at storytime or share a snack during a youth program—kids always get so excited seeing their principal or teacher outside of school! They would love to sit and listen to their high school idol read a story, or listen to a local "celebrity" talk about their job on TV or on the radio.

Steal These Ideas!

Invite a firefighter. One look at those uniforms, and the kids will be in awe! Have them answer questions about their jobs, and see if they're willing to let the children take a look at their vehicles and hear the siren. This is super simple (and free), but your young patrons will be talking about it for days afterward!

Show off a therapy or service dog. Is there someone with a therapy or service dog in your community? Invite them in to talk about how their dog has helped them. Animal visitors are always a huge draw for families, and you could turn it into a "hero animal" program, reading books and showing videos in which the pet saves the day. Serve animal-themed snacks—puppy chow, Goldfish crackers, Scooby Snacks (bone-shaped graham crackers), and animal-shaped fruit snacks—and you've got yourself a program.

Host a Human Library. You could also create your own version of a Human Library. This project originated as a way to encourage and facilitate open-minded, nonjudgmental conversations between people. These conversations can help challenge stereotypes and prejudices—when you "check out" a person from a different background or walk of life, it can lead to real change. See if any of your local heroes would be willing to be "books" in your Human Library, answering questions about their lives and participating in meaningful conversations with community members. (Note: If you want to advertise the event as a Human Library, you must first contact the official Human Library Organization to get permission to use their logo and materials.)

Track down your community's everyday heroes. Do you have anyone in town who is especially enthusiastic about volunteering? Maybe there's someone who takes it upon themselves each year to plant flowers all over the park, or someone who is famous around town for fostering dogs and cats in need of homes. Ask them to stop by for a program on volunteering opportunities in your community; if it's a children's program, the speaker could focus on how to become a hometown hero—go on a walk around town collecting litter, make blankets for animal shelters, create cards for veterans, and so on. A program like this would do wonders for showing young patrons that anyone can be a hero and that simple acts of kindness go a long way.

IDEAS IN ACTION

Storytime with the Fire Chief

CLEAR LAKE PUBLIC LIBRARY, Clear Lake, Iowa

The Clear Lake Public Library partnered up with the Clear Lake Fire Department for a very special storytime. The young attendees heard some stories, sang songs, and then ventured outside for the main event––the Clear Lake firefighters helped the kids spray the fire hose, let them check out the truck, and even took pictures with each child. What a wonderful way to showcase your community's fire department!

HELP THE LIBRARY, HELP YOURSELF

There's a chance that your family, friends, or members of the community may balk at being asked to do a program while getting nothing in return (unless, of course, your library can afford to pay them or reimburse them for mileage). Aside from the joy of the experience and the gratitude of the library, they probably won't really benefit much from doing a program for you. This is when you turn to local organizations that can stand to benefit in some way by partnering with your library.

Look for organizations that may have something to gain by coming to your library, since these are the ones most likely to participate for little or no cost. Consider organizations that want to spread the word about what they do. Various clubs are always looking to attract new members, and nonprofits are often open to finding new volunteers.

Humane societies, animal rescues, and shelters are always great partners for programs. Organizations like these are constantly in need of donations, volunteers, and adoptions, so they are often delighted at the chance to partner up with you and spread the word about the wonderful work they do. There are countless ways to collaborate; here's just a few.

Steal These Ideas!

Have a puppy party. Invite your local humane society director to bring a few adoptable puppies to your library and let patrons snuggle with them. The director can speak on the work the society does and why it's important, and he or she will hopefully leave with a few adoption applications or a few new volunteers. If it's a youth program, you could also go over proper dog care and how to approach a dog you don't know. For a craft, you could mix up some healthy homemade dog treats, make some human-only puppy chow for a snack, or create your own dog ears from plastic headbands and pieces of felt—easy and cheap!

Host a cat café. Cat cafes originated in Taiwan but are swiftly taking over the United States. It's clear to see why they're so popular—who wouldn't want to have a nice cup of joe and cuddle with some kittens?! Ask a local animal shelter if they would bring some adoptable cats or kittens to your library, and allow your patrons to book fifteen-minute time slots to go in and visit with the cats. It's best to keep your groups small so as not to overwhelm the cats. See if a local coffee shop might be willing to donate drinks or serve coffee for your patrons to enjoy.

Create items for shelter animals to enjoy. Got a lot of cardboard boxes? Create a luxurious cat castle! Tape some boxes together, and make cutouts for windows and doors with an Exacto knife, then let kids go to town with markers decorating it. Tied-edge beds are easy to make with some pieces of warm, fuzzy fabric and a bag of cotton batting, and cats and small dogs love them! There are tons of homemade dog and cat treat recipes out there, and cat toys are relatively simple to make: tie pieces of material around a hair tie to make a small wreath-like circle, or fold a cat treat inside a decorated cardboard toilet paper roll. If you can, have a volunteer or employee of your local animal shelter come by to accept these donations from your young patrons—they will feel so proud of themselves for doing a good thing for homeless animals!

Invite an environmental group or nature center. These groups are often happy to give presentations to libraries and schools—part of their mission is to educate the public on conservation and the environment. The best part of their presentations is that they often bring things for the audience to see, touch, or interact with. For that reason, nature centers are very popular with families who have young children—what kid doesn't want to peer into lake water to view tadpoles, see what's in an owl pellet (you don't want to know), or pet an animal? Nonprofits like these don't typically charge a fee, but they always appreciate a donation.

Create a summer wellness program. Local health centers or YMCAs often work with libraries to do wellness programs, and sometimes food banks donate food to libraries for them to have a free summer lunch program.

Create a connection with senior centers and day care centers. These places are often eager to work with libraries because it gives them an opportunity to do fun activities and build social connections, and everyone loves to see these types of partnerships in the news and on social media.

Put together packages for new babies. Local hospitals sometimes partner with libraries to put together a new baby package for new parents, emphasizing the importance of reading to your baby right from the start.

Contact local 4-H clubs or FFA programs. They generally have to have a certain number of volunteer hours each year, and they put on a great program!

IDEAS IN ACTION

Community Block Party

LORI JUHLIN, Hawarden Public Library, Hawarden, Iowa

A community block party is a great way to collaborate with other community groups and get people out and about in the community. The Hawarden Public Library in northwest Iowa held its first block party in July 2019, closing off two blocks, from the library to the corner of our community center and elementary school. Our children's staff reached out to community groups and businesses, seeking free and simple activities that could be done outside. The block party included inflatable games and a bounce house, sports games, face-painting, simple sidewalk games, sidewalk chalk, dance parties, water fights, a dunk tank, a selfie booth, and so much more! The community really rallied around the idea of a fun family-friendly event where games were free.

Our first block party was the work of our two part-time children's librarians, and it was planned in about three weeks. Due to these librarians' many community connections, it was possible for them to reach out and get participating organizations and businesses to sign on rather quickly. Those recruited included local businesses, school groups (like the football, baseball, and cheerleading teams), and community organizations like our Teen Center, Vacation Bible School, churches, and others. Public safety groups like the rescue squad and fire department also took part, and our dunk tank featured local community leaders like our police chief, teacher, pool manager, newspaper reporter, park ranger, and a local pastor.

In all, we had over 20 local groups take part, and well over 500 people attended the two-hour event one hot evening in July. Next year, we will probably recruit a few more volunteers to assist during the event so that staff can be freed up to check in with groups, provide water for workers, and ensure that everything is running smoothly.

Community Baby Shower

CHRISTY L. ROSSO, Sawyer Free Library, Gloucester, Massachusetts

As head of children's services at the Sawyer Free Library, I participate in a partnership with other local nonprofit organizations. We meet several times a year and support each other in group initiatives and programs. The public health nurse Kelley Hiland approached me with the idea of a community baby shower. We loved the idea, formed a small group, and got started with planning. We decided that the shower would focus on early childhood resources, maternal care, and family support. We would work with a six-month timetable, with steering committee members dividing tasks and meeting periodically, and we set a fall weekend date for the shower.

Gloucester, Massachusetts, is a seacoast city with a population of about 30,400. With nearly 120 to 150 births over six months, we planned for about 100 people to attend the shower. We limited the attendance to parents of newborns up to six months old and expectant parents with their families.

We invited area agencies to participate by setting up information tables at the shower. At the tables, health-related agencies such as local pediatricians, the hospital, city public health, insurance providers, and the La Leche League answered questions and described classes and referrals for free services. The YMCA offered family and infant/maternal classes emphasizing wellness. The following social service agencies came to the shower: Pathways for Children, Action Emergency Shelter, Help for Abused Women and Children, Open Door Food Pantry, Special Supplemental Nutrition Program for Women, Infants, and Children, and the Supplemental Nutrition Assistance Program. The Gloucester Fire Department demonstrated infant CPR and performed car seat safety checks.

The local food pantry catered healthy and delicious refreshments. Decorations came from a member grant. Children loved the lively music played as a donation by a local band. The library children's staff set up a special baby play area where YMCA staff helped with child care. Our staff welcomed older siblings and family members to the shower with fun games. One of our favorites was the Baby Food Taste Test! A local art organization, Art Haven, made a selfie booth with children where folks could pose for family photos.

We prepared gift bags for the new families with donations from our membership. We collected various raffle gifts from community organizations, like

FIGURE 5.3 / Community baby shower photo

gift cards and baskets from local shops, services from area businesses, and baby clothing and equipment. As she left the shower each mother/caregiver got a flower arrangement crafted through donations of flowers and vases.

We held a community diaper/wipes drive one month before the shower. We asked for all sizes of diapers, especially larger ones. The library and the YMCA had playpens to collect the donations. We gave everyone attending the shower diapers and wipes, and we donated the remainder to one of our member agencies.

Several organizations used grant money to buy shower supplies. The Friends of the Library helped with some of the shower's costs. Overall, our expenses were very low due to the many generous community donations we received. Twenty families registered to attend the baby shower. We recorded 225 folks that day, including all participants in the event.

Reading for Others: Summer Reading Partnership with a Children's Hospital

Program created by MARGARET MOHUNDRO and BARB DUNKLE. Program currently managed by DEANNA EVANS. Sanibel Public Library, Sanibel, Florida

Our library's summer reading partnership with the Golisano Children's Hospital of Southwest Florida began in summer 2011. The Sanibel Public Library Foundation wanted to participate in encouraging summer reading with the young patrons. Margaret Mohundro, the library director, suggested the "Reading for Others" program. She developed the idea after speaking to a patron who, with his wife, provided books to the children at their local hospital in New Haven, Connecticut. The Reading for Others program was born from this. Children who participate in this summer reading program read both to earn books for themselves and for patients at the local children's hospital. The Sanibel Library Foundation matches each book that each child earns with a book donated to the hospital. The spirit of giving is strong in Sanibel; the children were enthusiastic to earn books for children at the hospital, and the foundation supported the endeavor.

Books are provided to the summer readers by the library via its programming budget. The foundation provides the matching number of books, which are purchased through the Scholastic Literacy Partnership, for the children at the Golisano Children's Hospital of Southwest Florida. In 2016 the new youth services librarian, Deanna Evans, altered the program. Children read for specified amounts of time and/or complete theme-related activities to earn books. And since the Sanibel Public Library has a high level of visitors, she encouraged those children to participate as well. That year saw 204 participants in the Reading for Others program. In 2017, an online time and activity log platform was introduced for the children to use. When local children traveled, they no longer had to bother with a paper log, and when visiting children returned home, they could still log time to earn books for others. As of summer 2019, 307 children and teens had participated in the program, earning 1,284 books for over 2,200 hours of reading! So far, approximately 10,000 books have been donated to the hospital in total!

The community is always very supportive of the Reading for Others initiative. The children get very excited about earning books both for themselves and for others. Many visitors who participate in the program are on Sanibel Island for only a few days, and they will continue reading when they return home to earn books for children. Adult patrons and visitors have also been enthusiastic with their support, not only encouraging their young readers but even contributing to the foundation for the endeavor. We are so proud of our readers!

LIBRARIES HELPING EACH OTHER

When you're working in a small-town library, it's easy to view nearby libraries as your "competition." Often in rural areas, tiny towns are clustered very close together, and many families go to programs and events in multiple towns, not just the one in which they live. If you schedule your Halloween party the same day as the library a few miles away scheduled theirs, you'll probably notice a difference in attendance. But instead of silently fuming that another library is "stealing" your kids away, get together and work with them to make both library staffs' lives easier!

There are several ways to work with your neighboring libraries. You should e-mail one another regularly to keep up on each other's events and meetings so you won't schedule conflicting programs, or you can partner up and do programs together. This works especially well if it's a large event that your library may not have the space or funds to hold without help. By pairing up you can pool your resources, cut the cost in half, and use whichever building has the most space. You can also double your visibility by promoting one another's events.

Build other libraries up, and support them as much as you can—after all, you probably share most of the same goals, interests, and passions, so enjoy the things you have in common together. You can toss ideas back and forth, ask for opinions, and give advice when needed. Attend their events, and invite them to attend yours. Build that relationship, and you'll have a strong partnership for years to come!

IDEAS IN ACTION

Children's Concert at the Library

CHELSEA PRICE, Meservey Public Library, Meservey, Iowa

My library is *tiny*. I'm talking one large room, no meeting space, and if there's thirty people in the room, you're going to start sweating. But the theme for the summer reading program was music, and I *really* wanted to have a children's concert. And the band I wanted—Macaroni Soup out of Chicago—preferred indoor locations. What to do? Ask another library, of course!

The library that is only about five minutes from mine has triple the space of our library, and they use the same summer reading theme. So I reached out to see if they'd be willing to host the concert and split the cost if I took care of all the decorating and setup, and we got the show on the road! The concert ended up being a lot of fun, and we had around fifty little attendees having a great time singing and dancing!

NOW WHAT? THINGS TO CONSIDER AFTER PARTNERING UP

You've partnered up and created an amazing program, received great feedback from your patrons, and now you can relax . . . right? Wrong! You're not done yet. Henry Ford said that "coming together is a beginning, staying together is progress, and working together is success," and this means that you must continue to work on your business relationships if you want to continue your partnerships. Here's a few things to keep in mind as you nurture those relationships:

- Don't forget to revisit your partnerships periodically to evaluate and update your needs and goals.
- Always publicly celebrate your successes—post photos on social media and reach out to your local newspapers.
- Never forget to send a thank-you note, no matter how small the collaboration; if a business supplied juice boxes for a program, they should be getting a thank-you note.
- Find different, creative ways to recognize those who donated, assisted, or put on programs for your library—consider a monthly feature on your library Facebook page, an annual donor appreciation event, or a donor wall, if you have the space.
- Always make sure there are benefits for both parties— collaboration is a two-way street. If they help you, make sure to return the favor in some way.

All libraries are capable of being great partners, regardless of their size or budget. Partnerships help save money, nurture new relationships, and foster a wonderful sense of community, and these benefits cannot be ignored at a time when the very existence of libraries is sometimes called into question. Collaboration should become the culture of your library, not just a means to create a program; libraries must be so embedded in their communities that they are seen as essential and vital to their towns' well-being—the library should be part of every conversation about the community. Use your partnerships to help make your library—and *all* libraries—go viral!

6
Schools + Libraries = Programming Success

COLLABORATIONS BETWEEN SCHOOL SYSTEMS AND PUBLIC libraries are perhaps the most organic and natural partnerships that exist. After all, we share the same basic goals and initiatives when it comes to children—we want to instill in them a love of learning. We are both central to the community, and when we work together, everyone reaps the benefits. The natural synergy between libraries and schools points to the idea that "it takes a village"; both play a large part in nurturing children's love of reading and education. Partnering with schools is a win-win situation for everyone involved ... so why can it be so difficult to establish a successful connection with them?

School systems and libraries seem to be on the same team, but for various reasons, we often neglect to bridge the gap between us, and that must change. If your library has never tried to partner up with the school before, it can be daunting to take that first step. Who should you contact? What if they don't return your call? Why don't they seem interested? But once you cross that invisible line which has been drawn between schools and public libraries, you'll be so glad you did!

10 Reasons to Partner with Your School District

1. Share information and resources that the school or the library may not have known about otherwise.

2. Increase library card sign-ups.

3. Encourage new families to visit the library.

4. Inspire more kids to read.

5. Share your knowledge of new books with both students and teachers.

6. Promote the library's programs, services, and materials.

7. Collaborate on events.

8. Secure grant opportunities that wouldn't have been available to you prior to your partnership.

9. Expand the possibilities for events like author visits or field trips that your library may not have been able to afford.

10. Develop new relationships and connections with teachers, school staff, parents, and students.

WHERE TO START

Identify your person of contact. Sometimes your point of contact will be the school librarian, other times it might be the school's administrative assistant. The administrative assistant is often the gateway to connecting with other staff members. The assistant will know the correct person to contact, and she holds all the information as far as schedules, e-mail addresses, and other points of contact. You should also always contact the school principal or superintendent and introduce yourself. You don't need to have a specific project or event in mind right away—just reach out.

Here's a sample of an e-mail you might send to a school librarian:

> Dear Mr/Mrs. _____,
>
> My name is _____, and I am the _____ at the _____ Public Library. I wanted to reach out and introduce myself as we begin the new school year. I also wanted to offer up our services if you are ever in need--we have many educational resources, including (online research tools, e-books, etc.), as well as many materials that would be helpful to your syllabus. We would also be happy to help you in any other way, such as doing outreach, assisting with programs, or partnering up for an event. I look forward to collaborating with you in the future. Have a great week!

Pay a visit to the school. Once the school year has begun and things have slowed down a bit, stop by the school offices with some information about your library. Don't linger—just drop off some brochures, introduce yourself, and be on your way. Leave a few business cards with the administration staff, and encourage them to give the cards to teachers who might be interested in your services.

Attend PTA/PTO meetings. Attending these meetings regularly lets the public know that you are interested in and committed to bettering the community. You want to be seen as an equal partner with the school district, not just a place to go to check out books. Plus, you'll have a chance to get to know more parents, and when the parents are happy, everyone's happy!

Build an equal partnership. Once you feel comfortable enough with your points of contact at the school, make an effort to meet regularly—once a quarter, perhaps—to discuss any resource gaps in the school that your library can help fill, or vice versa. Your goal is to identify any problems that you and the school have in common and attempt to develop smart solutions to them. This could mean resource-sharing, collection-sharing, event-sharing/co-hosting, cross-promotion, collaborative grants—anything that could help the other party out. There has been a dramatic decline of school libraries and school librarians in the past several years, which is a huge detriment to students, so schools need public libraries' assistance now more than ever. Teachers often don't have access to the new titles that librarians do, so take every opportunity to share your latest books with them. Try to also get to know the school's reading coordinators/specialists and make yourself available to them. Be respectful and listen to their needs, and try to be low-maintenance and not needy—the school staff are often under a huge amount of pressure, and they don't need to add more to their already lengthy to-do lists.

SCHOOL OUTREACH

School visits are the bread and butter of library outreach. Doing outreach at schools has so many benefits. Not only are you reaching new children (and parents, if you attend a family event) and informing people about the library, but you also get the opportunity to engage kids in conversations about reading, which is so important. School visits allow you to do booktalks to students of all ages, giving them examples of amazing reads. When you do school outreach, you are communicating to students that reading is not just an in-school activity; it doesn't have to pertain to an assignment, and it's a pleasure rather than a chore.

Once you've reached out to someone at the school and gotten permission to do a classroom visit or attend a school event, build on that relationship and try to come to as many events as you can. Most libraries are already doing plenty of summer reading promo at schools, but try for more than that! It doesn't have to be anything too elaborate—outreach can be as simple as setting up a cart full of books in the school's hallway and letting students browse them between classes. Some libraries have had success talking to parents about upcoming programs or events at school pickup and drop-off—but if you try this, just be aware that parents may be in a hurry, so try not to bother anyone who looks rushed.

Think about other school-related events that could benefit from your presence. You could visit during finals week with some stress balls and coloring sheets (you could also try this at a university). If the school has an after-school program, see if you can visit monthly with a craft, game, or storytime. Does your library have a bookmobile? Set up a lending program with teachers and haul books to and from the school once or twice a month.

FIGURE 6.1
An easy storytime once a month is a great way to build
a relationship with your school district

As you can see, there are lots of possibilities for school outreach. Each time you visit a school, make sure you thank the teachers and staff profusely for allowing you to come, and never ask them for too much during your visits. Teachers and paras have enough on their plate, and they won't have any time to think of a craft for you or come up with something for you to do, so come prepared. (You know how exhausted you are after a hectic children's program? That's what their jobs are like *every single day*.) If you're able, try to find time to volunteer at school events a few times a year to give something back—no

7 Ways to Be Cool with Your School

Here are seven more school events that would work well with some sort of library involvement:

1. Parent nights
2. Open-house events
3. Literacy nights
4. Kindergarten roundup

5. Family reading night
6. School plays or musicals
7. Scholastic book fair

library promotion, just helping them out as a "thank you" for allowing you to build that relationship.

With school outreach, sometimes it's easiest to just find little ways for you to be *around*. Make an effort to introduce yourself and offer help to school staff members, and try to nurture those relationships as much as you can. You want to get to the point where you don't have to pester the school district to allow you to participate in events; instead, they'll contact you directly and ask for you to come. If your library doesn't have much extra time or staff, just do what you can. Just a few times a year can make a huge difference. When libraries and schools come together, everyone benefits!

IDEAS IN ACTION

School Sporting Event Outreach

JULIE ELMORE, Oakland City Columbia Township
Public Library, Oakland City, Indiana

Our first experience with a sporting event outreach program was a big one at homecoming. We set up our table, ran a running slide show about our e-books, and passed out swag. This was way back during the "Geek Your Library" event. Flash mobs were also a big thing at the time. So during halftime, we worked with the cheerleaders and grade schools and invited all the kids in attendance to come to the court at halftime and read for five minutes. The cheerleaders were reading with kids, and so on. Then the cheerleaders held up a sign reading "We Geek our Library" at the end. It was fun, and all we had to do was bring a couple crates of books over to have ready for kids to pick up and read. We then reminded them that all the books were available to borrow from the library, and we welcomed the adults at the game to get library cards for their children and come visit the library. We had a board set up at our booth as well about why they love the library, and it was fun watching it get filled up.

We also did a "Show Us Your Card" night at a high school football game. Anyone who showed us their library card or signed up for one got a cowbell or a ticket for a drawing for a prize. The cowbells were from Oriental Trading and were very popular with the kids.

OTHER PARTNERSHIP OPPORTUNITIES

Outreach isn't the only way to partner up with your school district. Here are a few different ways to make the most of the school–library connection.

Steal These Ideas!

Start a Reading Challenge. A little healthy competition never hurt anyone! See if the students can outread the school staff and librarians, then reward them if they do.

Build a school + library book club. The whole school reading the same book, along with your library, would make for some wonderful discussions and program opportunities.

Host a Battle of the Books. Participate in this fun incentive program where students compete with one another by answering questions about awesome books.

Combine summer reading programs. Save money, time, and energy by working with the school librarian or other staff to put together a joint summer program.

Participate in or host a faculty vs. student trivia night. Students will love competing against their teachers and library staff.

Host a school art gallery at your library. Work with your school district's art teachers to display student art projects inside the library.

Invite classes to your library. This is a tried-and-true way to work with the school district that requires very little effort on your part.

Host a teacher appreciation night at your library. Teachers work so hard; show your appreciation by hosting an event just for them.

Hold a Get Ready for Kindergarten program. Partner with teachers and school staff to provide an educational kindergarten preparation event for parents and their children.

Invite teachers to host a storytime. Ask teachers to read their favorite books to your storytime attendees.

Highlight a high school band, choir, or dance team performance. Invite various school clubs or groups to show off their talents to an audience at your library.

Build a buddy system with one-on-one storytimes. Pair high schoolers with kids who need a little extra help reading.

Even if your library has a one-person staff, you can still have a successful partnership with your school district. It doesn't have to take up a lot of time—even a half hour per month can make a huge impact. Every library is capable of having great collaborations with its schools; you just have to make an effort to reach out. When it comes to public libraries and school systems, together is better!

IDEAS IN ACTION

Popcorn & Paperbacks: A Public and School Library Crossover Book Club

TEGAN BEESE, Lake Villa District Library, Lindenhurst, Illinois

When I took over young adult services at the Lake Villa District Library, there was only a middle school book club. I expanded this by creating a young adult book club for grades 7 to 12, but eventually I felt that was too great of a range. I then split it up into a monthly seventh- and eighth-grade book club and a quarterly high-school book club. I chose to do the high school book club quarterly because those students are busy not only with academics but also with extracurriculars, such as sports and clubs, as well as family. I also tried to up the incentives to attend by providing paperback copies of the books to keep for those who register. Moreover, we read a book which has a movie connected to it that we can watch, and then we compare and contrast the two. Thus Popcorn & Paperbacks was born.

I reached out to the high school librarian, since we wanted to collaborate more on crossover programming. The high school had a book club that met every week, and they said they would be happy to have their participants read the same book as Popcorn & Paperbacks, so they could attend our program. They would meet once a week and discuss the book up to a certain point, and then attend our program at the end of the month (along with my other patrons) and we would discuss the book as a whole, and compare and contrast it with the movie to decide which one they liked best.

I not only have kids that participate from the high school in our district, but from surrounding high schools and homeschoolers. It is really great for them to meet people that they share similar interests with whom they might not have met otherwise. I even had two girls reconnect after not seeing each other since grade school camp. It was really fun.

My biggest cost is to provide the copies of the book to keep. I always try to do paperbacks, but have done hardcover once. It generally costs about $60 to get 10 copies of the book. As for snacks, we have a general snack budget that I and other book club programmers use, and we share the snacks. We spend about $50 when we buy new snacks, but that will last us for a few months of programming. I also check out the DVD to show, so I don't have to worry about purchasing a title. I'm able to show the title under our umbrella license that is purchased by the library. The program as a whole costs about $70 quarterly, so I am spending roughly $280 to do this four times a year.

The first Popcorn & Paperbacks program had 12 attendees; it was very exciting! This figure has ranged slightly since then, but I have never had fewer than 5 attendees. We recently read *Five Feet Apart* by Rachael Lippincott, and I gave out 14 of the 15 books I had ready.

My young adult patrons and their parents are all very excited about the program. They are always curious to find out what book they are doing next. I often have them bring their friends in to sign up for the program as well. The high school book club is a great way for kids to learn about this too, and I anticipate it continuing to grow.

D.E.A.R. (Drop Everything and Read)

SUMMER BELLES, West Pittston Library, West Pittston, Pennsylvania

Beverly Cleary first wrote about D.E.A.R. in her novel *Ramona Quimby, Age 8*, and since then, Drop Everything and Read programs have been held nationwide on April 12 in honor of Cleary's birthday. The official website celebrates all month long. The purpose of the celebration is to remind everyone to make reading a priority activity in their lives.

I arranged to do a D.E.A.R. event with our local elementary school. At the time, the school housed 450 kids, kindergarten through sixth grade. With the permission of the principal, I sent flyers home with every student to inform the parents that the program was taking place and at what time. I encouraged parents to show their support by driving by to "honk for reading" and sending their kids to school dressed in a particular color. I also wrote a letter to all the teachers thanking them for their time and cooperation, and I outlined how the event would unfold.

At a designated time on the scheduled day, an announcement was made over the school's sound system indicating the start of the program. Teachers instructed their students to grab a book, and then led them out of the building onto the school grounds. All the students sat and read for ten minutes. I was outside waiting and started a timer once everyone was out of the building. I signaled the end of reading time with an airhorn, at which time the teachers led their students back to class.

It was a huge success. The kids loved it, and the teachers thought it was a great idea. It became an annual event for a few years. I sent a press release to the local paper ahead of time, and they came to do a story on it, so it ended up getting a lot of community support and awareness. (Side note: The local photographer who covered the event entered a contest the following year using one of the photos from this event and won!) The best part is that this event literally cost the library nothing! We have a photocopier, so the flyers and teacher letters were created in-house, and I already had an airhorn, but any noisemaker will do.

Information Literacy Field Trip

SUMMER BELLES, West Pittston Library, West Pittston, Pennsylvania

The Information Literacy Field Trip was a yearly event that we did in conjunction with our local elementary school, hosting the fourth grade only. The goals of the trip were to introduce students to the library, get them familiar with its different sections, and teach them how to use the card catalog to find an item of interest. It required *a lot* of prep work and cleanup, but the cost was $0. We're a small library, so I could only host one class at a time (25–30 students), and I scheduled them to come in the morning before the library opened.

The field trip began with a tour of the library in which I explained the different sections, the difference between fiction and nonfiction, how items are arranged on the shelves, what the Dewey Decimal system is, and discussed any library lingo they would need to know (juvenile, spine label, call number, etc.). Then I broke the students into groups, got the teams set up at individual computer stations to access our online card catalog, and gave them their first item to find. I staggered the order of the sections between the groups so that I wouldn't have too many kids in one particular section. Their objective was to look up the item in the catalog, then go find it on the shelf. Once they did this, attached to the item was a slip indicating the next item to find. They ended up visiting just about every section to find all the items. When they were done, they were instructed to take the books to a table and look through them to pass the time until everyone else was finished.

BLASTT

CINA SHIRLEY, Douglass Public Library, Douglass, Kansas

BLASTT (Bringing the Library and Sisk Tweens Together) is a program that I started with the Sisk Middle School counselor in Douglass, Kansas. The program started in February 2017 for students in the sixth to eighth grades and is currently ongoing. Originally, I received a $500 new program grant from the South Central Kansas Library System for 2017. Since then, I have averaged spending about $500–600 per year on the program.

We have a program approximately every other month on a Friday evening when the library is closed. We have done activities such as cupcake wars, a bike scavenger hunt, "cocoa, cookies, and canvas," jewelry-stamping, an Easter egg scavenger hunt, and a Pop Tart taste-test challenge, just to name a few. We usually average 20–25 students in attendance. BLASTT has remained popular with the students because it gives them something to do on a Friday night in our small rural community.

7

School's Out for Summer

FOR MOST PEOPLE, THE WORD *SUMMER* EVOKES PLEASANT thoughts of lazy days and vacations. But for youth services librarians, the word can often bring on a rash, a bit of nervous sweat, and a stress ulcer. (I am *barely* exaggerating.) The summer reading program can feel like a never-ending treadmill of minute-tracking madness that you're ready to get off of. It can seem like you're constantly either getting ready for or recovering from summer reading. Some libraries spend the majority of their programming budget in those few weeks and then are left scrambling to put programs together for the rest of the year with the few bucks they have left over. Sometimes you reach the end of summer, exhausted and frazzled, and think, "Was it all really worth it?" It's so easy to burn out and forget to have fun throughout all of this.

For these reasons, the winds of change have been blowing when it comes to summer reading. More and more librarians are realizing that certain parts of the traditional summer reading program are "sacred cows" that need to be slain. Should we *really* be spending the majority of our programming budget on just 6–8 weeks of the year? Are prizes *really* a good way to reward reading, or are we just bribing kids who have no real motivation to read? Is it *really* a good thing for us to get to the end of summer feeling like we're going to die?

Read on to start exploring your reasons for doing a summer reading program, discussing what your goals are, and making little changes to improve the way you do things. You can learn to love summer again!

WHY HAVE A SUMMER READING PROGRAM?

Maybe you're reading this and thinking, "Wow, summer reading really is super stressful. Should we even be doing it at all?" Maybe you've read the research on forcing or bribing kids to read and how it doesn't work. Maybe you're so burned out you can't even bear to think about next summer's theme or what performers you can afford to book. Ultimately, though, summer reading in some form does have a lot of benefits.

BENEFITS OF A SUMMER READING PROGRAM

It fights "summer slide." You've most likely heard about the summer learning gap. When kids are on summer break from school, many of them aren't reading and learning daily, so when they arrive back at school for the next year, those kids are behind. The gap isn't equal—typically, lower-income students are at a disadvantage since they may not be able to attend costly educational camps or other activities. Libraries work hard to fight the summer slide, providing STEM programs and putting books into children's hands to help them enrich their minds over the summer vacation. Most libraries' ultimate goal in doing a summer reading program is to encourage young patrons to read and learn, and that in turn may help prevent summer learning loss.

It gets kids excited about the library. Part of the appeal for libraries to hold a summer reading program is to help kids see how great the library is. Of course, you have your regular young patrons who already know all about the wonders of the library, but summer reading is a time to attract new patrons and keep them coming back. Many kids (and parents) probably don't realize that you offer free programs and events on a regular basis, and summer reading is a great gateway into the library for new visitors. Turning one-time visitors into lifelong library users is another goal for libraries during their summer reading program.

It tries to improve kids' reading skills and stimulate their desire to read. It can be tough to find the line between encouraging children to read and bribing or forcing them to do so. When you find that line—using a minimal amount of extrinsic motivation and encouraging as much intrinsic motivation as possible—it's a beautiful thing. If you can turn even one nonreader into a reader through summer reading, you have done your job. It's also important to let young patrons know they have the freedom to choose whatever they'd like to read—an audiobook, picture book, graphic novel, comic book—it's completely up to them. It's not your job to police what level of chapter book they're reading; that is the duty of caregivers and teachers. The library's job is to help them find a book that appeals to them and makes them feel joy at the thought of reading it.

It provides opportunities for free family fun. Libraries have evolved so much over the past twenty years. No longer are they dusty buildings in which to hunt for a book; they now offer fun, exciting events and entertainment as well! A library is the only place you can check out movies and books, learn a new skill, watch a magician's performance, and bounce in a bouncy castle, all for free. Library programming is especially important in small, rural areas, where the community has to drive miles to see a movie, and in low-income areas. Nowadays, programming is just as important as the materials libraries offer, and the summer reading program is basically a programming extravaganza for all kinds of free family fun. Activities like these can also help draw in nonreaders, and once they're in the door, you can try to encourage them to leave with a book.

It increases interest in the library. Summer reading serves as great PR for the library. If you're in a small town, everyone has heard about your summer reading program, and chances are, there are flyers up everywhere. Summer reading events make for great photos, Facebook posts, and videos, and communities always love to hear about what's going on in town. A summer reading program boosts your library's presence in the community and helps you build traffic and circulation.

MAKE A GOOD THING BETTER

The intention of a summer reading program is wonderful—encouraging children to read and offering up a plethora of fun learning and educational opportunities. But maybe your library's summer program is a bit . . . tired. Maybe your numbers have dipped or maybe your staff is getting burned out. It's time for a change.

Change is a scary word for a lot of us. However, your patrons are so adaptable and open to it that they may not even notice when you trade out that cheap plastic junk for a free book as a prize, or if you nix hiring pricey performers and do a DIY science experiment program instead. We shouldn't fear change; what we should fear is staying the same, handing out the same minute-tracking sheet we filled out ourselves when we were young. Library programming should always be evolving, and fear of change is an awful excuse to not hustle for better results and happier patrons.

Maybe summer reading itself isn't a sacred cow, but parts of it definitely are. And maybe you don't have to burn the entire program to the ground, but it absolutely needs to be shaken up. Rather than getting stuck in the mindset of "Well, it's summer reading—we *have* to do it," try to shift your thinking to "Hey. Our new and improved summer program is almost here—I can't *wait* to show our patrons what we've been working on!" Here are just a few ways to reenergize, reinvigorate, and rebrand your summer reading program.

Assess your goals. What do you intend to achieve with your summer reading program? What, to you, is the most important part of the program? Is it the circulation numbers or the traffic through your door? Is it the variety of programming you offer? Is it the idea of getting books into more children's hands to encourage a love of reading? Or is it the chance to offer a summer program to pre-readers? Pinpoint what is most important to you, and then focus on that throughout the summer.

Rebrand. Some kids hear the phrase *summer reading program* and are immediately discouraged. Summer *reading* appeals to kids who already enjoy reading, but it doesn't attract nonreaders. Maybe they don't enjoy reading or being forced to read at school. Maybe they're not the best readers and feel anxious at even the *thought* of picking up a book. Whatever the reason, just the word *reading* can evoke some negative feelings. Some of your young patrons may have always steered clear of your summer programming because they think they're going to have to read, and they don't even want to get involved if that's the case. For this reason (and because summer reading programs are so much more than just reading books!), many libraries have opted to rebrand their summer reading program—some call it "summer learning program," "summer adventure club," or just plain "summer program." Get creative with your branding and see if more people respond positively!

Keep it simple. You don't have to do *all the things*. Tracking minutes read, having different levels of prizes, scratch tickets for teens, Bingo sheets for adults, a kickoff party, a wrap-up party, a weekly performer, *plus* daily STEM programs, storytimes, and summer lunch?! That is *a lot* for any library, much less a small library with only a few staff members. You don't have to hire performers at all, especially if you're working with a small budget, and you certainly don't need to do daily programming. If teen or adult summer reading programs never get good participation or feedback at your library, why are you still doing them? Cut them out to save time and energy, or simplify them to be less work.

The truth is, the summer reading program is what you make it. There is no rulebook saying that you *have* to track minutes read or that you *have* to hand out plastic toys that will most likely end up in the trash. You don't *have* to do something just because "we've always done it that way." Summer reading can be as intense and crazy *or* as low-maintenance and simple as you want it to be.

Are all of your programs during summer reading active, and do they require staff and take lots of time, money, and energy? Then cut back on those and increase your passive programming. Doing constant, intense programming can do a serious number on your energy and enthusiasm. Replace some of those costly, energy-intensive programs with passive programs or drop-in programs that require less work and less stress. You also don't have to have a kickoff party at all if it's sucking up a lot of time and money, much less a wrap-up party.

Choose a theme . . . or not. Many libraries follow a theme, whether it's the Collaborative Summer Library Program theme or a statewide theme. If you don't like the theme and it's not sparking any inspiration for you and your staff, *don't do it.* There's no rule that says you have to stick to that theme or that you even have to have one at all! Some libraries come up with their own theme or go completely theme-less. Whatever works best for your library will work just fine for your community, and your patrons will appreciate that your program is totally different from those of neighboring libraries.

Watch out for "We've always done it this way." Just because something has been done a certain way for years doesn't mean it's the *right way* to do something. That way of thinking leads to outdated policies and procedures, and libraries can't truly fulfill the needs of their communities if they never evolve. Conforming to this thought process also stifles creativity, and much of it might be due to misplaced nostalgia—we did this same summer reading program when *we* were kids, and so keeping it the same as "the good old days" makes us feel all warm and fuzzy. Yes, it's *easier* to stick with the old way of doing things, just coasting along, but you'll never get anywhere without taking a chance on new ideas.

Put books in hands. First of all, you can booktalk, booktalk, booktalk! Booktalk at your school visits, booktalk via video on your Facebook and Instagram pages, booktalk behind the circulation desk. There's a book out there for everyone, and it's your job to play matchmaker and find that perfect book for them. It's important to remember that summer is supposed to be fun for kids, and forced reading of a specific type of book is not fun. For this reason, try to encourage *all* forms of reading, including audiobooks, graphic novels, comic books, magazines, newspapers, and books of any level. It is not your responsibility to tell that fifth-grader checking out a picture book that she should be reading at a higher level, and it's not your job to tell that middle-schooler that he isn't old enough to check out a Stephen King book. Your job is to encourage a love of reading—*any* kind of reading.

Consider alternatives to tracking minutes read. Tracking kids' reading is tricky and a bit controversial in the library world. You want children to read for the simple pleasure of reading, not to win points and prizes. Tracking minutes, pages, or books read can lead to resentment on the child's part—reading may start to feel more like a chore or homework assignment than an enjoyable pastime. Librarians want to know that kids are reading, but you also don't want to suck all the joy out of it—it shouldn't matter how *much* they read, as much as the fact that they're reading at all.

Some libraries require that children or parents even write down the title of the book they read on their tracking sheet, which creates more work for parents *and* staff. This kind of tracking can also lead to dishonesty on both the child's *and* parents' part (yes, some parents will fudge the numbers to get their kid a plastic whistle, believe it or not!). Kids are also notorious for losing their reading logs—though if you're a tiny library, you probably know each kid's name and can keep the logs at the desk.

All of this has led to many libraries changing the way they track reading. Some don't do it at all. Others make up sheets or Bingo cards where kids can track not only their reading but other things as well, like making a craft, singing a song, volunteering, drawing a picture, playing a game, building something, or writing a poem. This is especially useful for kids who aren't reading quite yet—they can do many other things to earn points. Some libraries even give parents points in their own adult program for reading to their children.

You could set a community reading goal instead of an individual goal. If the community collectively reads so much, the library can have some kind of party to reward the whole town. Another option is to have a "patrons versus librarians" challenge to see if your participants can outread you and your library staff. Many libraries make their reading logs look different as well, turning them into packets, calendars, passports, or maps.

Be kind to your staff. If you're a director and have staff working under you, go easy on them during this stressful time of year. Allow them to wear more casual outfits and sneakers during the summer—it's hot, and they're probably on their feet for most of the day. Let them take a vacation if they have one planned. This might be frowned upon, but think about it—lots of weddings are in June, and if you have staff members with school-age children, summer vacation is really the only time they're able to travel with their kids. Many wonderful youth services librarians have actually transferred to other departments or left the field entirely because of all of the extra rules and restrictions placed on them, particularly during the summer, and it's a shame to see once-enthusiastic library staff members lose their sparkle because of burnout.

Ask for help. Make it known throughout your community that you are in need of volunteers for the summer reading program. Put up some flyers, and tell your favorite patrons—chances are, a few of them would be willing to help out here and there. Got a teen advisory board? Have them help out too! You could even contact the high school principal before school lets out for the year, and see if the school would be willing to offer extra credit to students who volunteer at the library during the summer.

Go mad with marketing. Summer reading has to compete with so many things—vacations, camp, family reunions, the list goes on. It can be hard to keep your numbers up. To increase your numbers, consider dropping your library card requirement if you have one—of course a visitor would need to have a card to check out materials, but they shouldn't need one just to participate in the summer program or attend a program. Also, if you still have a fine policy in place for overdue materials, maybe you should rethink that—many libraries have done away with fines for good. Often if a patron has an overdue fine, they will just never come back, and most libraries would rather have regularly visiting patrons than a few bucks for a movie that was several days late. Those two changes alone can really boost your numbers, and they don't require any work at all.

Summer reading is probably the thing that libraries advertise the most. Many libraries do school visits beforehand, which is a great way to get the word out to students. You can even check with school staff and see if you can bring in some other library staff and do a big assembly to reach more students at once. You could also consider partnering with other libraries in your community to advertise each of your programs together.

What's most important during a school visit is not the cool bookmarks you bring, or the amazing books you talk about (although those are definitely benefits!)—what's most important is your attitude. If you visit each classroom with an infectious energy and lots of enthusiasm, students will feel the same way about your program. Always have fun when visiting classrooms, and don't be afraid to make a fool of yourself.

Word of mouth is probably the most effective way to advertise your summer programs, particularly in a small town. Find a way to mention them to every patron who comes in the door. Promotional videos are also very helpful, and summer reading promos that make clever use of music often go viral.

If it's donations you're after—and what library isn't?—you can reach out to local businesses that might be willing to donate by sending them letters with return envelopes inside, to make it easier for them to send a check or coupons/passes for you to give as prizes. In your letter, briefly talk about the summer reading program and its goals, and tell a story about the program or your library that will make funders see how important that program is to the community. We'll talk more about getting donations in another chapter.

Regroup. Once the summer has come to an end, it's time to evaluate your summer reading program. How did it go? How do your numbers compare to last year? Did you feel you were getting more kids to read? What kind of feedback did you receive from the community? What did you like about the program? What didn't you like? Is there anything you would do differently next year? Take note of all of these things, and keep the information handy for when you're planning next year's program.

NO MORE CHEAP PLASTIC JUNK!

Librarians around the country have had enough of those summer reading prizes—you know the ones. The miniature flashlights, the flimsy toys that break almost immediately, the countless bracelets and lanyards sporting the summer reading theme. Libraries are tired of kids tearing through as many pages as possible to get that themed T-shirt, only to be done reading for the summer once they've earned it.

The truth is that offering prizes in exchange for time spent reading implies that reading is a chore that needs to be rewarded. Reading should be a reward in itself! Prizes serve as an extrinsic motivation for kids, while libraries should be making more use of intrinsic motivation (behavior driven by internal rewards), which tends to be more effective in the long run. A summer program should be about so much more than just earning free toys. For these reasons, many libraries have chosen to go prizeless during their summer programs. This helps young patrons see that reading and visiting the library *are* a reward—your collection is awesome, your free programs are amazing and entertaining, and your library is a warm and inviting space for kids to be themselves . . . That's a prize in itself! Other libraries have chosen other ways to offer prizes in exchange for pages read—here are just a few ideas to change your summer prizes.

Steal These Ideas!

Put together science activity packs. A huge number of libraries have started offering "activity packs" as incentives during their summer reading program. The packs are given out in Ziploc baggies and include materials to do a science experiment or craft, along with a printed sheet of instructions. The activities are simple and include inexpensive materials that many libraries would already have. For example, a marshmallow architect activity would include mini marshmallows and toothpicks. A balloon rocket activity includes a balloon, a piece of string, and a plastic straw. A science experiment activity pack includes ingredients for slime/oobleck or vinegar and baking soda. A gardening activity would include seed paper, potting soil, and instructions for planting. You can find so many great ideas on Pinterest, and it's not hard to keep it simple and cheap. These packs are a great way to get the kids to actually *make* their own prize, and then they're learning without even realizing it.

Think up some experience prizes. People often remember great experiences more than they remember material objects, so why not offer some awesome memories as your prize? Maybe if your whole group reads a certain amount, they get to go on a field trip or have a pizza or ice cream party. If your staff is up for it, kids could win movie nights, lock-ins, slumber parties, or after-hours events. A prize that will be remembered forever by your young patrons is a ride in a fire truck if they reach a certain reading goal. If you're really brave, tell kids you'll dye your hair, or let them throw a pie in your face if they reach their goal.

Offer "bragging rights." Some kids would love nothing more than for all of their friends to know that they are "important" at the library—give them a reason to brag with a sign in their yard (with permission from their parents, of course), allow them to ring a bell in the library when they've reached their goal or announce it over the speaker, or let them choose their favorite book in the library and personalize a bookplate with their name.

Consider literary prizes. A book as a prize makes the most sense for a library, whether it's discarded or donated. Make it clear to the kids that this book is theirs to keep forever, and that often ramps up their excitement. Some other literacy- or learning-based prizes could be an activity book (think crossword puzzles, riddles, and word searches), journals and pens, magazines, bookmarks, book bags, and so on.

Offer coupons or passes. A good way to partner with various community businesses or organizations is during your summer reading program. Ask them if they would be willing to donate coupons or passes to your library. Many businesses will agree because they know that if a child receives a movie pass, for example, parents will most likely bring the child and then pay for their own tickets at the theater. You can visit places like McDonald's or Dairy Queen for vouchers for a free ice cream cone, and check at places like bowling alleys, aquariums, zoos, bakeries, roller skating rinks, and so on. This is also a great way to advertise the various attractions in your town.

Even though there are many good alternatives to traditional summer reading program prizes, don't feel pressured to change if the ones you already have are working for your library. If the prizes are always a hit and you feel like they encourage reading in the long-term, that's great! Some prizes which always seem to be popular are food (snacks and candy) and gift cards, particularly with teens. Many libraries also find fun ways for patrons to find out they've won—a prize wheel is fun for any age to spin, and scratch tickets are super popular. Even if they scratch the ticket to reveal "Not a winner," just the act of scratching the ticket is often enough to make kids and teens happy!

IDEAS IN ACTION

Summer Reading Program

REBECCA MCCORKINDALE, Gretna Public Library, Gretna, Nebraska

When I started working at my library over a decade ago, I quickly learned one thing: the summer reading program = chaos. By the time I'd survived a second summer, I knew that things needed to change. And by my third summer, I was in a management position and could actually work with our library team to reimagine what our summer programming should look like.

We wanted the focus to be on making good memories, and we had already laid a foundation for that with our coupons from local businesses—we just needed to kick this up a notch. I came up with the idea of a booklet in which kids are rewarded for their weekly reading activities by coupons in the booklet.

When a child brings in their booklet, we look for a reading time listed, and then we "activate" the coupon on that page by stamping it with our library's logo. We provide suggested reading times broken down by age/grade in the booklet's instructions, but what we really want is to encourage the enjoyment of reading for its own sake, instead of making it a chore. At the very end of the program, if a child has read every week, then they get to pick out two books to keep. We happen to have a Scholastic Warehouse about ten minutes away, and so we go to their sales, and we have gone through their online system as well.

Each year's booklet centers around the Collaborative Summer Library Program's theme, and every year we call the booklet something new such as a "passport," "dream journal," or "mission log." My husband donates his time and talent to create a themed version of our library's mascot (a dragon). These are touches that both our patrons and businesses love seeing—what the theme is and what our booklets look like.

Over the years we have really honed in on what works for both us *and* our community. Our summer reading program is now the opposite of chaotic, and you can tell that it has a special place in both kids' and their parents' hearts. You can get more details about this program on my blog Hafuboti.com. I have two posts there that go into more detail in what we do and why—one from the early stages of the program, and a more recent version, where I even include our Publisher files, which you can use to make this program your own. I encourage you to take a look at your programming (summer or otherwise) and analyze it to see whether or not it's serving your community in the most useful and efficient way.

Summer Reading Refresh

ADRIANE HERRICK JUAREZ, Park City Library, Park City, Utah

Starting in 2016, the Park City Library in Utah took on the challenge of changing our summer reading program to make it easier, more fun, and more engaging for everyone in our mountain-town community. We thought about the many ways people can fuel their interests through the library in the summer. Reading is part of that. But what about mastering 3D printing, learning a new language, starting a journal, practicing public speaking, or finding out the best ways to train your dog? Inspired, we threw out plastic prizes, reading trackers, and sign-ups and changed the name of our program from Summer Reading to Summer Challenge, making it an all-ages, interactive program.

As summer heats up, our librarians activate a partnership with a local art center's teen camp, where teens design an interactive art project that is installed in the library for the season. Participants in the reading program interact with the art to set a goal they want to complete during the summer. For example, the 2019 Summer Challenge theme was "Literacy through

Letters." People wrote their summer goals on postcards and put them in a flowered mailbox that the teens had created. These were then mailed back to participants at the end of the summer.

The time and money that was once spent on prizes and trackers now goes into developing inspiring programs. Coming to the Park City Library in the summer might include listening to live outdoor concerts, doing yoga on the library patio, taking part in improvised fairy tales, listening to bilingual stories, taking part in writing workshops, engaging in tech tutoring, or learning to play the ukulele.

"We give away free books at every program," says the children's librarian, Katrina Kmak, "and we talk to families about the importance of keeping their brains active in the summer months to avoid the dreaded 'summer slide,' which for students often means losing learning. But we don't dictate *how* they must do that. We invite them in, let them set their own goals, support them, and then watch the library come alive with activity. It's been a huge success!"

FIGURE 7.1
Interactive art piece: Literacy through Letters

SUMMER LUNCH

Though summer lunch programs for children have been offered at religious organizations and schools for quite some time, libraries have been the most recent institutions to jump on board with this great cause. That's right— though food in the library was once frowned upon, it's now a regular occurrence. In small rural communities, schools or food banks aren't always within walking or biking distance for kids, so libraries saw this need and filled it. Now, kids under eighteen (and sometimes their caregivers as well) can visit many public libraries and get a free, nutritious lunch during the summer.

In many small towns, the poverty level is fairly high, and kids are often left to fend for themselves in the summer while their caregivers are at work During the school year, they would have regular healthy lunches, but now that summer has rolled around, their meals may be more sporadic and not as nutritious. These kids often end up at the library during the weekday, making library summer lunch programs a natural fit. Hunger creates a barrier to learning, so kids with empty bellies have a difficult time enjoying all that the library has to offer.

While some libraries take on a summer lunch program all on their own, others partner with local churches or school districts to do this. If the nearest school is located in a different town, see if the school will allow a bus to come pick up children from your library to take them to and from meals. Some libraries even partner up with local assisted living homes, which share their

6 Benefits of Lunch at Your Library

1. **A library is non-stigmatizing.** Since the library is a welcome space for everyone, no matter what their age or income is, it is a neutral and inconspicuous place for people to come for free meals.

2. **Patrons don't have to prove themselves "worthy" of a free lunch.** Libraries will allow you to have a free lunch without asking any questions (besides maybe "white or chocolate milk?").

3. **Help combat summer slide.** Not only do summer lunches at the library help with the summer nutrition gap, they help with learning and literacy as well.

4. **Welcome new families to the library.** Introduce yourself to new faces, explain what your library has to offer, and talk about the programs you have that are free and available to everyone.

5. **Open doors for new community partnerships.** Some organizations in your community may be interested in donating toward the wonderful cause of a summer lunch program.

6. **Increase your library's visibility.** When media and news outlets hear about your library offering summer lunches, they will probably be interested in doing a story on the program!

meals with the library. You can also contact the Summer Food Service Program, which is part of the U.S. Department of Agriculture. They do have pretty strict rules as far as leftover food, cleanup, and food storage go, so that's something to consider.

It's nice to be able to offer fresh meals every day of the week, but if you're a small library doing everything on your own, you may only be able to handle a meal one or two days a week . . . and that's perfectly fine! That's two days when these kids are getting healthy, filling meals that they may not have gotten otherwise. If this is your situation and you're feeling overwhelmed, ask around for volunteers to help you serve and prepare the meals. One person can't do it all, and there's no shame in asking for help.

IDEAS IN ACTION

Love in a Lunchbox

CINA SHIRLEY, Douglass Public Library, Douglass, Kansas

Love in a Lunchbox is a program that was started in summer 2017 with the elementary, middle, and high school counselors, the local churches, the Ministerial Alliance, and the Douglass Public Library. We are a low-income community, and there is a need to feed the children and their families during the summer. Every Thursday, one of the churches sets up tables and chairs on the lawn outside the library and serves lunch to children and their families. The families are also given food to take home with them. We received a grant and also asked the community for donations to start this program.

We meet at the end of each school year to discuss how much money there is for the program, and then we divide up the weeks between the various churches. Afterwards, the middle school counselor and I will make a trip to the Sam's Club in Wichita and buy food and supplies for the program. Each week, whichever church is serving will decide what they want to serve that day, and they also put together sack lunches for the families to take home, with items that were bought at Sam's. In summer 2019, Love in a Lunchbox fed approximately 200 children and adults. The program is still going strong and the churches, school counselors, and the library will continue to feed families in our community that are in need.

My Experience with a Summer Lunch Program

CHELSEA PRICE, Meservey Public Library, Meservey, Iowa

I just started a summer lunch program at my library in summer 2019. The nearest free lunch program was at a school twenty minutes away, and many of the young patrons who visit my library in the summer don't have transportation available—they're riding their bikes around town all day. Many of them come in to the library as soon as we open and are there until we close, and they almost *always* beg me for food. I would give them popcorn and bottled water, but I didn't have much else to offer.

Seeing how hungry these kids always seemed to be, I started to kick around the idea of starting a summer lunch program myself. I was curious to see if any local restaurants or businesses might be willing to partner with me or donate food, so I put some feelers out on a local Facebook page.

The feedback I received from this post was overwhelming. I had teachers sending me messages wanting to drop off snacks and friends interested in giving me gift cards for the program, but the vast majority of the feedback was from complete strangers. Many of them shared about their own childhood, when the summer lunch program in their own neighborhood was something they depended on, and how some days they would not have eaten if it wasn't for that free lunch. Around 25 people reached out to me asking if they could donate, and 20 of them were people who had never even met me or visited my library.

The post ended up getting some attention from local media, who came to the library with cameras and did a story about the program that evening on the news. We ended up with over $2,500 in donations. Two of the donors wrote checks for $500 apiece; neither of them were people I knew, nor were they from the town my library is located in. This just goes to show that you never know who might be interested in donating to something.

At this time, I was staffing the library by myself. Our library assistant had just retired, and I had not yet hired a new one. I decided to serve lunches on Mondays and Fridays, and I decided to do it all on my own. (Note: Don't do this. You need help.) The program was for kids eighteen and under, and I made sure to advertise in a way that was non-stigmatizing, saying that everyone would be welcome, no questions asked.

The first day, no one showed up—and I was very nervous that all those people had donated for no reason. However, 4 kids showed up the next time, and the rest of the summer we had between 2 and 12 kids for each meal. I read them picture books while they ate—the age range was so vast that we couldn't agree on a chapter book—and we served things like veggies and dip, apple slices, sub sandwiches, and macaroni and cheese.

The kids seemed to really enjoy the program, and they rarely left food on their plates. On the last day of the program before school started, we had a pizza party, and the kids continue to ask me almost daily if we could have "free lunch" all year round. We ended up having some donated money left over, which we used to purchase backpacks and school supplies to give away to kids who needed them. I hired my new library assistant halfway through the summer, and she was a huge help when serving the food and cleaning up.

There are a few things we will think about doing differently next time. I am going to look into partnering with our school district to save on costs. We never could have done a program like this without donations or grants—it's just not in our budget. I will also put a call out for volunteers; preparing and plating the food can be quite stressful to do on your own when there are hungry kids waiting. I also hope to make the lunches into more of a "program," integrating chapter books and maybe an activity after they've finished eating.

Overall, we considered the lunch program to be a success. Whether it is two kids we're feeding or fifty, it makes no difference—those are two kids who are going home with a full belly and a smile on their face! We will definitely be making summer lunch a regular thing, and hopefully we can do it more often than just two days a week. If my tiny library is able to pull it off, *any* library can!

GO FORTH AND CONQUER SUMMER!

Whether you call it summer reading, summer club, summer adventure, or summer fun . . . don't get the summertime blues! Be careful not to put absolutely everything you have into your summer program because honestly, libraries should be doing amazing programs all through the year—it shouldn't *only* be about summer. If you feel yourself burning out, pull back and take a breath. Consider reaching out to your fellow librarians—you are not alone, and only another librarian can truly understand the exhilaration and exhaustion that is summer reading.

Remember, what you are doing is important. You are making a difference in many lives. Always remember that. Don't get caught up in numbers—sure, it's great to see circulation and attendance steadily increasing, but even if you reach just *one* child who hated reading and now loves it because of your hard work, it's all worth it. Summers may seem like your Everest, but you've made it to the top time and time again, and you will continue to do so.

8
Take Chances, Make Mistakes, Get Messy

YOUR PROGRAMS ARE GOING TO FAIL.

Take that in, and take a deep breath. It's going to be okay.

It seems like every librarian's worst nightmare, right? The craft is ready to go, the snacks are prepared, and you've got your programming director hat on and a hopeful smile on your face. You're prepared for a huge turnout. The event has received great feedback from the community, and you can't wait to see it through. You are the best, the most *amazing* librarian in existence. And then . . . it happens.

Nobody shows up.

Sound familiar? You're not alone. Virtually every library employee out there has felt exactly what you're feeling. You're probably wondering what you could have done differently, why no one was interested. You might even be feeling that *you* are the failure. It's easy to get down on yourself. But it's important to remember that just because a single program failed, that doesn't mean *you* failed. Sometimes you can do everything exactly, perfectly right . . . and the event still doesn't work out.

That's just life as a library employee—some of your programs are going to suck: either no one shows up, only a couple of patrons attend, or your attendance is decent but the attendees don't seem to have a good time. No matter what you consider to be a program "fail," what matters most is how you react and learn from these mishaps. Are you going to wallow in your feelings of failure, swearing never to try the program again? Or are you going to pick yourself up, laugh it off, and take an even *bigger* chance next time? I think you know the answer.

YOUR PROGRAM FLOPPED . . . NOW WHAT?

You've worked *so* hard on prepping for an event, and the community seemed supportive. Maybe a few patrons even requested the program. But still: zero attendance. This can be disheartening, particularly when you were responding directly to a patron request or community need. It's depressing to look around an empty room with a table of untouched crafts and a plate of uneaten cookies and wonder where you went wrong. You poured your heart and soul into this event . . . for nothing! But hold on—take a beat, and regroup using the following steps.

Reframe. Are you thinking negative thoughts? *What a dumb idea, no one wants to come to my programs, what was I thinking?* Well, stop it right now! These thoughts are not helpful; they're only making you feel like crap. Reframe those thoughts: *I did everything right, everyone has off days. I'm proud of myself for making an effort.* Make a joke out of it: *Guess I'll just eat those cookies all by myself!* You are your own worst critic, and your value as a librarian is not affected by one program that didn't work out. Thinking more positively and laughing at yourself will almost immediately get you out of your funk.

Ask questions. Why do *you* think this program flopped? If it was attended, however sparsely, what worked? What didn't? How many people attended? What would you do differently next time? Ask yourself these questions after every library event. Better yet, keep a document with all of this information for future reference, whether it's in a binder or an Excel spreadsheet. By keeping track of your programs—both successes and failures—you'll be able to refer back to your document in the future and see patterns. Maybe you typically have low attendance in December, and by looking back at your document, you'll decide to take a little programming break during that month. Or perhaps you'll see that for whatever reason, Thursday nights don't tend to work well for your book club. We can't always predict when and what programs will work, but this document can give us a better idea.

Share your failures. Join a few librarian Facebook groups or discussion lists, and share your experience with a group of people who understand. It's almost 100 percent guaranteed that they've all been there, and they will commiserate with you and maybe even offer some advice. You know deep down that if you're not failing, you're not trying, but your fellow librarians can remind you of this maxim.

Don't compare. Maybe comparison isn't the thief of joy, but it doesn't make you feel great when you see that another library in a town twenty miles from you recently did a program very similar to yours, and it brought in dozens of patrons. *How come they could do it and I couldn't?* you might be wondering. Again, reframe—every library is different. Maybe that town has a school and yours doesn't, or maybe they did more advertising than you did. Whatever the reason, it doesn't matter. Other libraries are not your competition, and it won't do to obsess over comparing yourself to them. There will always be another library doing something bigger, cooler, more impressive—root for them, be inspired by them, and learn from them.

Try, try again. Get back on that horse and try it again! Look back at your notes from the event, and see what changes you could make this time around. Don't completely discard a program that you think is great just because of low attendance. Remember that J. K. Rowling was rejected twelve times before someone finally decided to publish *Harry Potter*, and look at her now! (Sure, maybe publishing a book isn't quite the same as planning a program . . . but it's something to think about!) Being a successful programming librarian is a marathon, not a sprint, and great things take time. So tweak your timing, do some more advertising, or target a different age group, and fail forward by learning from past mistakes.

6 Possible Reasons for a Program Flop

Nine times out of ten, the reason for low or no attendance is not a lack of interest in the program, and though there's no one way to ensure consistent attendance, you should always give it another try using what you've learned. After all, failure is only temporary, and chances are you'll do better next time. Here are six possible reasons for a flop:

1. **Bad weather**—Check that forecast!

2. **Perfect weather**—If the sun is shining and it's a beautiful day, families might make other plans.

3. **Timing**—It could be too close to a holiday, or it could be church night. Maybe there's a big basketball game or a school event that is conflicting with your program.

4. **Advertising**—Did you forget to put a flyer up in the post office or send it in to your local newspaper? Advertising can have a huge effect on program attendance.

5. **Age**—If you're in a small town and are constantly have trouble getting teen attendance, maybe it's simply because there aren't that many teens in your community. Try the same program for older kids and see what happens.

6. **Structure**—Sometimes parents and families prefer a drop-in program instead of an active, structured program; it allows for more flexibility.

MOVE ON

We all fail. It's a part of life. We cannot grow as librarians, as humans, without failing a few times in the process. Being innovative, being creative, being an impactful librarian practically *requires* failure once in a while.

Don't dwell on your mistakes; learn from them. Without that empty storytime, you might not know that you shouldn't plan kids' programs at 3:30 p.m. because they don't get off the bus until 4:00. Without that failed social media event for teens, you might never have learned that most young adults no longer look at Facebook, and you should offer programs on Instagram or dare to sail the uncharted waters of TikTok. So don't feel bad. Before you can focus on making it right, you have to learn what's wrong.

LEARN FROM MY MISTAKE!

During one of my first years as a library director, I planned a "puppy party" program that I was very excited about. There was an adorable craft, cute dog-centric decorations, dog breed trivia, and on-theme snacks all out on display in (unused) dog bowls—there were cheese balls as "large-breed kibble," Reese's Puffs cereal as "small-breed kibble," Scooby Snacks graham crackers as "dog treats," and Twizzlers as "chew toys."

It was the cutest thing ever. My dog-loving husband, who often helps me with programs, and I waited to watch the kids stream through the door. No one showed up, not one person! What I should have mentioned before is that the aforementioned "puppy party" was centered around Animal Planet's annual program *Puppy Bowl*, which is shown immediately before the Super Bowl. Because I care far more about puppies than about football and have no interest in pre-gaming myself, I assumed there would be others like me. I was wrong. In small-town, rural Iowa, nothing can compete with football!

At first, I was devastated, but then my husband and I decided to make a joke out of it and do the program ourselves. We made dog-ears out of felt and a headband, played the games, and yes, ate the snacks out of the dog bowls. We took funny pictures and later posted them on social media, joking about what a hit our program was. People got a kick out of it and gave a lot of feedback on what a good program it should have been.

FIGURE 8.1

One of the silly photos taken when no one showed up

In retrospect, it was silly of me to try to swing a program on Super Bowl Sunday, but hey, we learn from our mistakes! Sometimes the only way to learn is to try and fail.

TAKE THAT RISK!

So now you've tried, you've failed, and you're not afraid anymore. Right? You're ready to take a *huge* leap and do a *big* program that you've *never* done before. Right? You're prepared to pull off an event that could rival any big-city library with a *much* larger budget than yours, and you're going to rock it! Right? Right. So let's go!

If you've ever attended a library conference as a small library, you've probably found yourself thinking, "*My* library could never do that!" Even at a conference for small libraries, you might still feel like a fish out of water (the word *small* varies wildly from library to library). Maybe you went to a presentation where they talked about spending $500 on Nerf guns for a single teen program, and you started sweating at the thought of asking your board for such a thing. Or maybe the session on escape rooms left you feeling overwhelmed and discouraged. "We don't have the budget, the staff, the time, the space," you thought. "We can't do that!"

But here's the thing: *You can.*

In this section, you'll read about several small libraries that made a large-scale program on a small budget. These are libraries that were not afraid to take chances and make mistakes; they may have started off by thinking "This wouldn't work at my library," but eventually they stopped thinking of their smallness as a lack of something. When you read about their programs, I hope you'll walk away feeling inspired and empowered to take your own leap.

IDEAS IN ACTION

Author Elizabeth Berg Visit

CHELSEA PRICE, Meservey Public Library, Meservey, Iowa

When I started as library director, I made a list of programs, fundraisers, and events that I wanted to plan at some point. About halfway down the list I wrote "Elizabeth Berg book signing––LOL." That's "LOL" as in "That's hilarious. Why would a best-selling author visit our little library?" Little did I know that only a few years later, I would be welcoming Elizabeth Berg herself into our tiny town.

I've been a fan of Elizabeth Berg's work since I was in high school, so when I saw on her Facebook page that she was doing a Midwest library tour, I was excited at the prospect that she might be speaking nearby. I noticed that she wasn't visiting any Iowa libraries, and even though it seemed like her schedule was finalized, I decided to send a brief e-mail to her partner and media escort, Bill Young. I told him a little about our library and how important it is in our small town, and I said that if they were ever in the area on another tour, I would love to toss our hat in the ring.

Not five minutes later, the phone rang. "Hi there, this is Bill Young," said the voice on the line. "I just received your e-mail as I was sitting down to look at Elizabeth's tour schedule. We have an open day before we head home. Would you like to be our last visit on the tour?" Needless to say, my excitement could not be contained, and of course I said yes.

Before I got too excited, I had to let Bill know just how small our library really was. There would be no separate meeting room, I told him, no fancy microphone and speaker system—just one big room filled with folding chairs and a small podium. He reassured me that small towns and libraries were Elizabeth's favorite, and that it wouldn't be a problem. With that, the Meservey Library was on the schedule.

Thankfully, Ms. Berg did not charge a fee for this particular tour. Without her gesture of goodwill, we probably would not have been able to play host; needless to say, our budget doesn't really allow for author visits. She only asked three things of us: that we have treats for our attendees to enjoy, that we display some beautiful flowers here and there, and that we try to partner with a local animal shelter to have an adoptable animal in attendance. The local humane society director was more than happy to bring two small adoptable dogs to the event.

I immediately posted a request on social media for any small, local bakeries to contact me about making baked goods for the event. To my surprise, I was contacted by five small businesses which were happy to donate cookies, cupcakes, and doughnuts at no cost as long as I put out business cards acknowledging them. I also called a local florist about getting a few arrangements. She refused to accept payment; she was very excited about the library getting a visit from such a big author and wanted to help. With these donations, the only things the library had to purchase were plates, napkins, coffee, and lemonade.

Clearly, it was very important to advertise this event well; we didn't want Elizabeth Berg to show up at an empty room. So I contacted local radio stations, newspapers, and TV news. I created a flyer and e-mailed it to all the other public libraries in my district, asking if they would be willing to help me advertise. Most were more than happy to do it.

We ended up having eighty attendees. This might not seem like much to larger libraries, but our little building could not have held one more person; it was the best-attended adult program we have ever had. People came from hours away to hear Elizabeth speak, and the feedback I received was wonderful. Elizabeth and Bill (and their dog Gabby!) could not have been nicer or more complimentary of our town and library.

FIGURE 8.2
Elizabeth Berg with some of the library staff and board

There is no doubt that this event wouldn't have happened without good timing and a whole lot of luck. The fates were on my side. However, it also would never have happened if I hadn't reached out in the first place. I honestly didn't even expect a response from Elizabeth Berg, but I figured no harm could come of a simple e-mail. The lesson to take away? Don't be afraid to reach out and ask. Maybe you'll get ignored, maybe they'll say no . . . or maybe you'll end up having your best program ever.

Our Library Comic-Con

CASEY PETIPAS-HAGGERTY, Maynard Public Library,
Maynard, Massachusetts

The Maynard Library hosted its first annual library comic-con in November 2016. Attendance at large commercial comic and fandom conventions in the area had been growing exponentially, and other libraries across the country had successfully run library comic-cons. We have a large graphic novel and comics collection, a comic book expert for a director, and several self-proclaimed geeks on staff. Why couldn't we host a library comic-con ourselves?

We had a small but ambitious schedule for our comic-con the first year and have been adding events and activities to it every year since.

Every year, we have:

A comic book author or illustrator—so far they've all presented workshops, but that is always subject to change.
Super Hero Training Camp—Pinterest has been a great source of ideas for this!
Video Gaming—we've been incredibly lucky to have the support of a local gaming shop to make this possible.

Scavenger Hunts—there is a Pokémon-themed scavenger hunt every year, and we've also had Dragon Ball, Harry Potter, Disney, and Infinity Gauntlet-themed hunts.

Photo Booth.

Poster Board Polls—these are poster boards that we label with an opinion question. Attendees are welcome to vote either by using dot stickers or by writing their answer directly on the poster board. In the polls, we've asked participants about their favorite fictional character, what superpower they would most like to have, Xbox vs PlayStation, their favorite Ninja Turtle, their favorite Justice League member, Jedi or Sith . . . the options are endless!

We also make sure to change the schedule of events a bit each year. There have been various types of trivia programs, a Harry Potter–themed Bingo game, a Lego program, crafts, and an escape room. Finally, we invite a comic bookstore and any interested local comic book illustrators and authors, artists, and novelists to set up a table in our very small artist alley.

The most expensive part of the day is the author's honorarium. So far we've hosted local authors who have been affordable in part because they are local, including Jef Czekaj, Shelli Paroline and Braden Lamb, and Jason Viola and Zack Giallongo.

A local gaming and comics store provides the equipment and manpower for the gaming program, and other local businesses donate prizes. Most of the decorations and program materials are made in-house or use items that a staff member or the library already has. For example, the "weight" at the Super Hero Training Camp is made from two Cool Whip containers, duct tape, and a wrapping paper tube, and the stuffed animal that trainees must rescue comes from the play area in the Children's Department. We used a home Bingo game owned by a staff member for the Harry Potter Bingo, and one year we filled three display cases with action figures, Lego sets, and collectibles owned by staff. The prizes are often donations from local businesses, like new book donations to the Friends of the Library book sale or leftover prizes from the teen summer reading program.

Overall, this has been a highly successful annual event. We get an average of 150 to 200 people through the door specifically for comic-con activities, and our circulation of graphic novels and comics rises significantly the month of the event. There are always several families and individuals that remain at the library from the start of comic con at 10:30 a.m. to the end at 4:00 p.m., and the attendees include children, teens, and adults of all ages. It's an event that can grow and change as the fandom interests in our community change, with new fandoms being included and others being dropped, and it's an event we and our patrons look forward to every year!

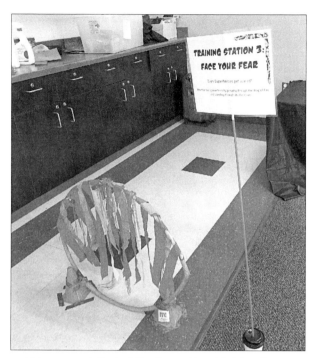

FIGURE 8.3 / Part of the Super Hero Training Camp

"Stranger Things" Escape Room

CHELSEA PRICE, Meservey Public Library, Meservey, Iowa

An escape room was one of those things that I thought was out of the question for a library as small as ours. For one thing, we don't have any separate rooms to lock people into; our entire library is just one large room. Where would attendees escape from? Plus, escape rooms are complex, high-tech, and expensive; it would be impossible to pull one off in a tiny library, right? Wrong!

After attending a webinar on library escape rooms, I decided to give it a try. I had just hired an enthusiastic library assistant, and we were both big fans of the Netflix show *Stranger Things*. The third season had recently wrapped up, and we figured it was the perfect time to do a program based on the show.

It was so much fun to come up with different puzzles and clues for the escape room. We used things like hidden ciphers, using a UV flashlight to find an invisible message, and we even buried a clue inside a tub full of slime!

A key step in planning our escape room was to draw out a map and write down our plan. Having a step-by-step practice walk-through of the room was extremely helpful. Planning an escape room is a lot of work, and it's easy to get confused when trying to figure out which clue leads where. We also had my husband be the guinea pig and play through the room, timing him to see how long it took him to escape.

Details can make or break an escape room. Since *Stranger Things* is set in the 1980s, we had a blast finding different props to scatter throughout our room. We decided to make the back of the library look like a 1980s basement hangout, with a ping-pong table, a TV, an Atari game system, and movie posters everywhere.

We actually didn't have to buy any props at all. I had tons of props at my own house—a ceramic ET figurine, 1980s board games, books, the video game system—and what I didn't have, I borrowed. We printed a bunch of posters and advertisements from businesses featured in the show, and we even made labels for New Coke to tape over regular Coca-Cola cans.

Another fun detail was our photo booth. We taped up some paper and decorated it with printed-out monsters and references to the show, and we made props using paper and Popsicle sticks. We took photos of our groups after they escaped and put them on our social media. My library assistant also baked some *Stranger Things*-themed cupcakes, which our attendees loved!

One of my favorite things about the escape room was that the clues led participants outside into our shed. We had emptied out the shed previously, so all that was inside for players to find was a (very creepy) Jack-in-the-Box which had a clue inside it. What they didn't know was that there was also something else waiting for them outside: my husband in a borrowed Demogorgon mask! He tapped on the windows while they were in the shed and chased them back into the library. We did warn attendees—all teens and adults—that there would be a jump scare, and they were all fine with it and ended up *loving* it. The players seemed to enjoy that element of surprise, and it was fun to hear them laugh and scream. The best part was, it made for some hilarious footage on our outdoor camera.

We did purchase the Breakout EDU kit several months before our program. The kit costs $150 and is full of different locks, a UV pen, and other helpful ways to create an escape room. You wouldn't have to purchase this if you don't want to; you can find many different kinds of locks on Amazon. You can also check with your local school district or other community libraries to see if they have a kit that you could borrow for a week or two. We decided to purchase it because we're planning on doing more escape rooms in the future. Other than the Breakout EDU kit, we purchased quite a few black plastic tablecloths from Dollar Tree. We hung these up throughout the room to make it dark and add to the effect of being in the Upside Down. That was all we had to spend money on. Everything else was either borrowed or belonged to us. The setup was simple, but the program was at night, and the room looked great in the dark, with only flashlights and Christmas lights to guide the way.

We ended up having three groups of six attend our escape room, and that was perfect for us. We needed hour-long slots for each group (45 minutes for the room and 15 minutes to reset the room), so we would've had to extend it another night if anyone else had signed up. Those eighteen people had a *great* time and thanked us many times for the program. All three groups escaped with just a few minutes left to spare.

Since our library is just one large room, we had to do the escape room in the back section of the library. Luckily, we have a wooden screen that folds across to separate the back section from the front, so the illusion of being in a 1980s basement still worked. We used walkie-talkies to communicate with players if we needed to, and they could ask us for three clues throughout the game. Technically, we could've just shouted to them from across the library and they would have heard just fine, but the walkie-talkies added a fun, nostalgic touch. We also set up two baby monitors in the room, so we were able to hear and see the attendees as they moved through the room. This was very helpful for us, because we had to time the Demogorgon's "attack" just right. It was also fun to watch the participants try to work through our puzzles.

Overall, we consider the escape room a great success and can't wait to do it again. It was a *lot* of work and took a lot of setup time. However, it was all worth it to hear the attendees' excited voices as they stumbled across a clue and see their triumphant happy faces when they managed to escape! So if you're in doubt, just know that if our tiny library can do it, yours can too.

FIGURE 8.4 / Photo Booth

Summer Carnival

CHELSEA PRICE, Meservey Public Library, Meservey, Iowa

Meservey has always had an annual Fireworks Day a few days before the Fourth of July, and the library had never been involved . . . until two summers ago. That's when I was approached by someone in the fire department who was wondering if the library might want to participate.

I'm pretty sure they were expecting me to plan a storytime with a few crafts and maybe a snack, but my response—for whatever reason—was "I want to plan a carnival!" I had no idea what I was getting myself into. It would turn out to be more than worth it, but who knew a carnival would be *so* much work?

I started by fundraising. A local bank gave us $750 toward the carnival, and we were able to raise another $850 by doing a baked potato bar fundraiser. When renting inflatables and carnival games, I asked for discounts wherever I went; most people said no, but some said yes, and that was a success in my book.

I found a local family who were willing to bring some goats, rabbits, and donkeys for a petting zoo at no charge as long as they could put out some 4-H information, which I was more than happy to do. A local butcher who is known for his kindness and generosity provided hot dogs—300 of them!—at no charge. The town bar owner offered to donate bags of chips and ice for the snow-cone machine we rented. Board members donated things like condiments for the hot dogs, packages of soda and water they found on sale, and paper plates.

With all of these generous donations, I barely had to spend any money on this event. The two most expensive things were the rented inflatables ($850 for three pieces) and the insurance that we had to have for the petting zoo ($550). However, these expenses were completely covered by the bank donation and our earnings from the potato bar fundraiser.

I ended up purchasing the following with library programming funds: snow-cone syrup (cheaper on Amazon), temporary tattoos and face-paint, several prizes to give away (I found deals on Amazon and Target Cartwheel), one grand prize (one year a tablet, the next year a drone—I found deals on Black Friday), bottled water, hot dog buns, two carnival game rentals, and a few décor items. That was it! In all, we spent about $300 from our programming budget.

I am lucky to have a crafty family; my brother built a water balloon slingshot for the event, as well as a ticket booth that we used as a photo backdrop. My sister-in-law made an adorable elephant that doubled as a donation box. Our high school dance team volunteered to do the face-painting and temporary tattoo applications, and many community members showed up to help set up, serve food, and clean up after the event.

FIGURE 8.5 / Carnival

The day before the carnival, I was afraid that no one would show up and all my hard work would have been for nothing. There ended up being nothing to worry about because it was a *huge* hit. We had 300 attendees the first year and almost 400 the second year—more than the entire population of our town. The entire event was free, but we had a donation bucket by the food as well as the donation elephant. The first year, $750 was donated; the following year, $1,200. That is huge for a town like ours!

I received the most amazing feedback, and it was clear that an event like this was badly needed in our community. The carnival is now an annual event that my patrons talk about frequently. Even though it's a *lot* of work, I love seeing how happy it makes the town.

Laser Tag in the Library

Program created by KATHERINE GRIMM-BOWERS and ADAM NOVITT; currently managed by KATHERINE HAND and HEATHER MCGUIRK. Sunderland Public Library, Sunderland, Massachusetts.

The Sunderland Public Library has hosted "Laser Tag in the Library" programs for teens and tweens aged 11–18 since 2014. Teens are invited into the library during its closed hours for a team game of Laser Tag. They run through the darkened library, hide in the stacks, and think of creative strategies to get their team the win. The library uses Nerf Lazer Tag Phoenix LTX Taggers, purchased through Amazon, for the program. No other equipment is required, since the game is played with just the laser phasers. We initially purchased four sets of two phasers, allowing two teams of four to play against each other each round. Besides the initial purchase of the laser phasers, the only other costs for this program are batteries for the lasers and staff time. We set up the

Young Adult room in our library as the "safe zone," where teens can retreat to reload their phasers, take a break, and socialize while they are waiting for their team's turn to play.

The goals of this program are to provide a social opportunity for teens, provide a means of physical activity (especially during our long, dark New England winters), and help teens develop a relationship with the library beyond their normal expectations. We've found that the most exciting aspect of this program for most teen participants is the fact that it takes place when the library is closed to the public. The idea that the library is open just for them and that they get the chance to run around wild in a building where they are generally expected to be calm and quiet is very fun for teens. It allows them to develop a new sense of what a library can be and what role it can play in their lives.

The biggest challenge in hosting this program is finding a way to do so that does not condone violence. Our head of Young Adult Services always starts the program by discussing the rules of the game, encouraging the teens to work as a team, and making sure that everyone knows they can retreat to the "safe zone" whenever they need to. We are also extremely cautious about how we advertise this program to our community. We use the terms "laser phasers" and "blast" instead of "laser guns" and "shoot," and we never use images depicting teens pointing a laser phaser at the camera or at one another in our flyers and press releases. We have had community members complain about the inherently violent nature of the game, so make sure that your director and board of trustees approve of this program, and have your justification prepared in case of community complaints before you begin hosting this program.

WhoCon

DAWN ABRON, Zion-Benton Public Library, Zion, Illinois

https://teenservicesdepot.wordpress.com/

Comic-cons are all the rage, but who said you have to limit a con to comics? You can tailor any con to your demographic. Con means "convention," so patrons expect to see a variety of activities, including crafts, cosplay/costume contests, games, and prizes. Cons can be as long as you want. Some cons are the typical two hours, and some last for two days.

Our library has a lot of patrons who are into *Doctor Who*. We figured this out by asking teens to fill out a short survey during our regular school visits. We listed every popular fandom, including *Harry Potter*, *Game of Thrones*, *Supernatural*, and anime/manga, and we asked teens to circle their favorites. *Doctor Who* was the most popular one after *Harry Potter*.

At our "WhoCon" we offered a lot of different activities, all referencing the show:

Life-size Guess Who with *Doctor Who* characters

Re-creating *A Starry Night* with the TARDIS—participants had to re-create the *Starry Night* painting from the Van Gogh episode.

Gallifrey name buttons—we used a name-converter website and made the conversions into buttons.

Green screen photos—attendees chose one of two pre-selected pictures to use as their background, and their pictures were printed for them to take home.

Scavenger hunt—we hid pictures of The Silence all over the library. Participants received a five-clue sheet and took a selfie with each Silence they found. They showed the activity leader their five pictures in exchange for Jelly Bellies.

Doctor Who trivia—we created two 20-question trivia games using Kahoot.

Bowtie craft—this was a simple bowtie craft using felt. Attendees were given key chain holders, earring backs, and pin backs for crafting.

Costume contest—a photo was taken of all the participants, and all non-costumed guests were encouraged to vote using stickers.

The most popular activities were the Gallifrey name buttons, the Kahoot trivia, and the Van Gogh *Starry Night* re-creations. We had a total of 75 participants, and the entire program only cost the library $120!

6 Tips for Big Program Success

1. **Leave your comfort zone.** It can be scary to try something new and unpredictable, but it is so worth it!

2. **Ask for help.** There's no shame in asking for help, and volunteers will often jump at the chance to help bring something new and exciting to the community.

3. **Don't burn out.** If you don't find help and try to do a huge event all on your own, you will burn out! Be careful, pay attention to how you're feeling, and take your breaks and vacations.

4. **Eliminate the word "can't."** "I can't do this at my library." You *can!* Almost any event that a huge library does can be modified to fit a smaller library.

5. **Advertise!** It is necessary to advertise heavily for your new or large-scale programs if you want a great turnout.

6. **Ask, ask, and ask again.** There is *no* harm in asking for help, for discounts, for a favor. It's better to have taken that chance and gotten turned down than to have never taken the chance at all.

9

Mo' Money, Mo' Programs

IN MANY SMALL RURAL LIBRARIES, YOU ARE FORCED TO THINK hard about every financial decision you make. Can you afford to book that pricey performer for your summer reading program? Should you really be subscribing to magazines if only a couple of people are reading them? Do you *need* to have snacks at every event? Every dollar counts, and you must stretch that dollar as far as you possibly can, particularly when it comes to programming.

It can be difficult for libraries to even cover their operating costs, salaries, and material expenditures, much less program supplies, guest speakers, and author visits. Sure, lots of libraries have a Friends group behind them, but most still have almost no programming budget to work with. Sometimes you are forced to beg, borrow, and steal in order to have decent programs at your library.

So what's the answer? How can you write a grant proposal that will have a foundation throwing money at your library? What are some great fundraiser ideas that haven't been done a thousand times before? And what is the best way to ask people for money without seeming pushy and annoying? In this chapter, we'll discuss all of this and more, and hopefully once you've finished reading, you'll have all of the tips, resources, and tools you need to go out and get that cash!

COMMON MYTHS ABOUT ASKING FOR MONEY

Funders only care about numbers. Of course having great numbers is a plus when appealing to donors. But numbers are definitely not the only thing taken into consideration. Nothing hooks donors like a great story. Libraries are nostalgic for many people; there is typically a lot of emotional appeal when libraries are brought into the conversation. Use that when asking for donations. The message to send is that libraries change lives, build communities, and are worth investing in. Think stories over statistics—people are more likely to give when you can make them feel something. When asking for donations from the public, telling them that program attendance numbers are up 30 percent probably won't mean much. However, telling them about the senior patron who rarely leaves his house but attended a recent program and was the life of the party? That just might hit home.

How I feel about my library doesn't really matter when it comes to funding. It sure does! When you're making an ask, your attitude is of the utmost importance. If you don't believe in this project that you're trying to get funded, donors will pick up on it. You must have an unwavering faith in the value of your library and the project; you must believe that libraries are more important now than ever and that your library in particular is worthy of support. Even though asking for money can be awkward and can take you out of your comfort zone, you need to have confidence in yourself and your project, as well as confidence in the donor's willingness to give. These are all things that people can pick up on and that can make or break your proposal.

Large foundations are the only ones that will give a lot of money. Actually, individuals have proven themselves to be the biggest donors. And don't forget that several small grants add up and are usually just as worth applying for as large grants. This is why libraries should fundraise beyond the typical donors—seek out small local businesses, and build relationships with organizations. Many places that you don't think have the ability to give actually *do* give, and most of them are interested in helping out the library to benefit the community. You probably know about your community foundation's grants, and you might even know that Walmart gives out small grants, but what about your local gas station or mom-and-pop grocery store? Does your area have a local co-op? Ask them for a grant, and you'll probably end up getting it. You never know what businesses or organizations might be willing to donate, and the worst they can do is say no.

If our library does one big fundraising event a year, that's good enough. Wouldn't that be nice? Unfortunately, that's not the case. Fundraising should be a year-round activity for public libraries. Sure, you can have that one big event, but you should also be constantly applying for grants and writing grant proposals. You should always have some kind of ongoing fundraiser going on that doesn't require much upkeep. And keep up with holidays and important dates—try to get some media-savvy patrons to share your Facebook fundraiser on Giving Tuesday (the Tuesday that follows Thanksgiving) and see how much your followers give. At the end of the year, send out appeal letters; for many people, the months of December and January are when they do most of their charitable giving.

Everyone knows that libraries are always getting their budgets cut. You would think that most people understand how public libraries are funded, but a lot of them don't! You'd be surprised how many people are under the impression that libraries have more than enough money to function, and they have no idea that the majority of libraries are struggling. For this reason, it's important to get out there and ask for what you need. If you don't ask for it, you aren't going to get it; your community can't help you if they aren't even aware that help is needed.

It's rude to ask for money in person. It doesn't have to be this way! Learn the art of the ask: first, choose your timing. Don't approach someone while they're at dinner and start yammering about the library. It's best to start a conversation like this in a face-to-face meeting that you've scheduled, or at some kind of networking event. Also, choose your person wisely. Make sure you have a relationship with that person and aren't just contacting a random stranger. Start with pleasantries rather than just coming right out and asking. Then, make the connection between the person you're speaking to and the library. Appeal to their emotions by bringing up a memory they might have of the library, and stress the importance of the library in your community. Finally, explain your specific need and make the ask. Don't be vague—shoot straight and tell them exactly what the library is looking for.

Here's an example: "It's so nice to see you, _____; thank you for agreeing to meet with me! We've had some really great feedback on our 'Author Q & A' program, and I know that was something you enjoyed attending yourself. It's so nice to be able to offer things like this to our community, and I really think our patrons get a lot out of it, since there is nothing similar offered for free anywhere nearby. We would love to start an 'Author Q & A' series, rather than just a single program, but the cost just isn't in the library's budget. Each author charges a _____ fee to visit. The library is able to cover the cost of snacks and coffee, but we really need some help for the author fees. Is there any chance you would be willing to sponsor an author? We would put your logo on all of our advertising, and we would make sure you're recognized in the local news media. What do you think?"

Hopefully, the answer will be a resounding *"Yes!"* In that case, thank them profusely, be sure to send them a thank-you note, and thank them publicly once the donation is in hand. However, if they say no, don't worry. Thank them for the time they spent meeting with you and tell them how much the library appreciates their patronage (assuming they are a library user). Don't pester them again—if they change their mind, they'll contact you. Even if they aren't interested in donating money, maybe they would be interested in donating volunteer time or supplies in the future.

The only people who donate to libraries are the people who use them. Nope! Actually, many people with the ability and willingness to donate aren't library users at all. Just because someone doesn't enter the doors of your building doesn't mean they don't support the library. That's why it's so important to get out into the community and advocate for your library—advocacy, outreach, and fundraising all go hand-in-hand!

START WITH THE CITY

If you're a public library, the chances are you get a large chunk of your funding from your city government. And if you're a smaller library, chances are that it doesn't seem like *enough* funding. Maybe you haven't had an increase in years, or maybe you just think it's time for a bigger jump in your annual increase. Either way, you need to build a good relationship with your city council if you want them to consider giving you more money.

Ask yourself the following:

- Do you know your mayor and council members by name?
- Do you attend council meetings regularly?
- Are you keeping the city informed about the offerings and events at your library?
- Have you invited council members to any events at your library?

If your answer to any of these questions is no, then you should start doing that thing. If it's your job to request funding from the city, then it is *critical* that you work on building those relationships. You don't have to invite the mayor to lunch or anything—although it certainly wouldn't hurt!—but getting your city officials to think positively of you is important. Remember that those are the people who make decisions about your library's funding.

You should be at meetings (even if the agenda does not pertain to the library), ready to tell the city council how your program attendance has been steadily increasing or that you received wonderful feedback on a recent storytime. Sure, they might act like they don't care—tell them anyway! Keep them informed of any unexpected income (grants, donations, etc.) you've obtained, and personally invite them to big library events. Encourage them to stop in to check out your recent update of the children's area, and remind them that your meeting space is always available for use if they need it. Ask their opinion on things; make them feel important. Attending council meetings is the best way to keep up-to-date with things that are going on in town that could affect you—you need to know what's going on in the community.

Volunteer for community events that have nothing to do with your library, and try to get to know your elected officials. Send them Christmas cards during the holidays. It may feel a little weird at first if you aren't used to being so friendly with your city council—some city/library relationships can get quite contentious. But if it means that your library could get a sizable funding increase or more community support, why not do a little schmoozing? Getting yourself a seat at the community table just might open the door to amazing opportunities.

The truth is, even though the library and the city are not one and the same, they are nonetheless a team working together to improve the community. If you always keep communication open, invest your time and energy in working with them, and never look at the city as the "enemy," everyone ends up winning—your library, the city, and your community as a whole.

An important rule that you should keep in mind when requesting funding (and just getting along as a library employee in a small town) is "relationships first, money second." You should form relationships not only with the city council members, but also with the school employees, the editor of the local newspaper, and even the old men who gather for coffee at the gas station every morning. Not only is this great for attracting potential donors, it's also just plain common sense—more people will want to come to your programs if they have a nice relationship with you.

You should simply find ways to be around—have dinner at the local watering hole, attend school functions, join a local club, or start one of your own. You want people to be talking about you and your library (in a good way)! It's so important in a small town to not only establish trust with the community, but also to remain positive and upbeat when you're out in public. Someone is always watching you, so even when you're feeling "off," you still have to be "on." The more enthusiastic and excited you are about your library and your programs, the more people will want to come (and possibly donate).

BEYOND BOOK SALES

Ongoing fundraisers like library book sales are great. However, book sales have come to be pretty commonplace in libraries, and while they're a great way to get rid of weeded books, they don't tend to be big moneymakers. Before we get to fundraising events, let's talk about some other ongoing fundraisers beyond book sales. These kinds of fundraisers, while not cash cows, are a great way to bring in a little extra money to help with, say, the cost of materials or library décor.

Steal These Ideas!

Adopt a book. An adopt-a-book program allows patrons to give a donation to the library in order to "adopt" a book—a personalized bookplate will be put inside the cover of the book, signifying the person who adopted it. Many patrons like to adopt books in honor or memory of someone who has passed away.

Make a "coins for coffee" donation box. Does your library have coffee available for the community? If you haven't already, put a small donation box beside the coffeemaker and empty it out at the end of each week. You might be surprised at the amount. Similarly, consider putting a spot for donations at the front desk—if you'd like, you can make it fun by using a wishing well or a coin funnel.

Offer an option for online donations. Amazon Smile is something to consider—ask your patrons to select your library as their chosen nonprofit, then do their Amazon shopping like they would normally do. Upon checkout, the Amazon Smile Foundation will donate 0.5 percent of the purchase price to the library. Crowd-funding sites like Kickstarter or Indiegogo are also worth looking into if your library is trying to raise money for something specific.

Sell library merchandise. Have some T-shirts, tote bags, or other merchandise printed with your library's name and logo, and sell them for a bit of profit throughout the year. If you've got a button-maker, create some visually appealing buttons with your library's logo and put a price tag on them. Not only will you be getting a little extra dough, there will also be plenty of people out and about repping your library on their clothing!

Put together a community cookbook. Gather tried-and-true recipes from members of your community and compile them into a cookbook. This will take a little extra staff time and effort, but it will pay off—everyone loves cookbooks, especially one that includes recipes from people they know! Along the same line, you can sell calendars throughout the year featuring different photos of community hot spots.

Offer donor-funded décor. Does your library have a cobblestone walkway or stones bordering a garden? Consider letting folks "adopt" a stone, paying a fee to have their name engraved or painted on a stone in the walkway. Donors could also pay a set amount to be added to an art installation or wall decoration of some sort, featuring the names of community members who have donated.

Create a library wish list. Wish trees are especially popular around the holidays, but why not all year-round? Include items that the library needs or wants, and let patrons choose which item to donate. You can also keep a running wish list on your library's website, Amazon page, or social media pages. And don't forget to include a "donate" button on those pages as well, in case people would rather donate money than an item.

Set up a donation can. Partner with a local business or organization to see if they would be willing to have a library donation can in their building. People who visit their establishment may not set foot in the library but are still interested in donating. You just never know—those who want to donate might not even be library users at all!

Consider non-event fundraising. There are also some fundraising ideas that don't require much work on your part whatsoever. For example, put some feelers out to see if any local restaurants or businesses would be willing to partner with you for a weekend to have a portion of their proceeds go to your library. Several libraries throw an annual "Stay Home & Read a Book Ball," where introverts who would rather not attend a big event but still want to donate to the library can send in donations from the comfort of their own home. These "non-events" are a playful way to raise funds, and you can pair them with some social media extras as well—a live Q&A, reader's advisory, and a photo contest where your patrons post photos of themselves cozy at home with their books.

IDEAS IN ACTION

Class Photo Album Fundraiser

CHELSEA PRICE, Meservey Public Library, Meservey, Iowa

In a corner of our library building, we have a display of poster-sized senior class photos from the school that used to be across the street from the library, years 1927 through 1956. Many people enjoy looking at them and finding relatives, but the photos are awkward to look at and are in a seldom-used part of the library. The director before me decided to scan these photos and print them off as more reasonably-sized 5 × 7-inch pictures. She ordered some cheap photo albums from the Dollar Tree and put the photos inside. After getting a few requests from patrons for their own albums of these photos, she decided to make it an ongoing fundraiser. Ever since then, the albums have sold like hotcakes! The people who grew up in Meservey go out of their way to tell old friends and family about the albums, and we've even been asked to make some for people who live across the country. The albums sell for $10 each, and while it doesn't make us much money, it's enough to pay for the albums and photo paper and then some! The feedback we get from happy patrons is good enough for us.

Coin Vortex Funnels

REBECCA MCCORKINDALE, Gretna Public Library, Gretna, Nebraska

The Gretna Public Library has two small coin funnels at the front desk. They have been used for various things in the past, including a Cats vs. Dogs poll—one funnel represented "Team Cat," the other "Team Dog," and patrons would drop a coin in to vote. It was a huge hit, and people came into the library just to vote! During Random Acts of Kindness Week, the funnels were used to collect donations to pay off lost item fines for random patrons. The week had a "Giving Tree" theme, so the funnels were turned into miniature bonsai trees with a small sign explaining the goal. Once the trees got onto social media, even people from out of state contacted the library requesting to help pay

FIGURE 9.1 / Giving tree

for some of the lost items! This helped pay off many people's fines, and those patrons were thrilled. It also started some wonderful conversations between parents and children about the importance of helping others.

SIGNATURE EVENTS

Now let's put the "fun" in "fundraising" and talk about signature fundraising events! A signature event is pretty self-explanatory—it's a unique program that is typically successful and well-attended, and it's the event that your library is best known for. When people hear the name of your library, maybe they automatically think of your annual summer carnival, or your Halloween "haunted library" event. Signature events are great for generating recognition for your library, increasing positive attention, and giving your patrons something to look forward to every year. For these reasons, establishing a signature fundraiser is a no-brainer!

4 Reasons to Try a Signature Fundraiser

1. **Fundraising = friend-raising!** With a large event, there's a chance you'll end up meeting people you've never met before.

2. **Raise the library's visibility in the community.** Signature events can help put your library on the map.

3. **Partnership opportunities.** Meeting new people means new possibilities for a partnership.

4. **Reinvigorate.** Signature fundraisers can energize and reinvigorate you, your staff members, your trustees, your volunteers, and your community.

Steal These Ideas!

Put together a golf tournament. Typically, various businesses will sponsor a hole on the golf course for a sum of money, then each player will pay a fee to play in the tournament. You would have to negotiate with the golf course to figure out how exactly the library would get the money and how much—will the golf course donate some of their earnings for the tournament to the library or would the library only receive the hole sponsorship fees?

Host a talent show. Talk your patrons, family members, and friends into performing their talents in front of an audience, then charge a small fee or free-will donation for the community to attend.

Organize a 5K Run or a Fun Run. The participants pay a fee to run, and sometimes businesses sponsor the event so that the library can provide extras like T-shirts for the runners and prizes to the winners. You can also include a children's race for a shorter distance, or create a story walk for walkers to enjoy.

Host an ice cream social. Purchase ice cream and toppings (or seek out donations of them from small local businesses), then ask for a free-will donation from your community at the ice cream social. Who doesn't love ice cream?

Hold a bake sale. Chances are, you have several patrons who just love to bake. Ask them if they would be willing to whip up their favorite recipe to donate to a bake sale fundraiser—with bonus points if they include their recipe for attendees to take home!

Host a pancake breakfast. A breakfast event is a simple and fairly low-cost way to raise money for your library. See if your board members or Friends of the Library would be willing to donate food items—syrup, butter, sausage links, and so on—or donate their time to help cook.

Organize a community garage sale. Collect unwanted items from your community, then hold a library-wide garage sale.

Offer Santa Claus photos. During the holidays, many parents look for places offering Santa photos for a good price. Make that place your library! Create a photo backdrop and enlist the help of a staff member with a great camera or, better yet, a local photographer who is willing to donate their time. Ask for free-will donations instead of a fee and you may be pleasantly surprised at how much you end up with!

Host a dance party. Host a 1950s sock hop, a 1980s prom, a preschool prom, a daddy-daughter dance, a zombie prom, or any other number of themed dances, and charge a fee to attendees.

IDEAS IN ACTION

Superhero Program Series

REBECCA VERNON and VERONICA GROESBECK,
Anamosa Library & Learning Center, Anamosa, Iowa

Anamosa is a community of 5,533 in eastern Iowa, and due to our rural location about 30–50 minutes from any larger city, our community members always want more things for kids to do in town. Our director and our youth services librarian are both huge Marvel Cinematic Universe (MCU) fans, so we put together a spring-long, superhero-themed program series for all ages, called "What a Marvel-ous Spring." This series culminated in a private showing of *Avengers: Endgame* at a movie theater in the nearest city, Cedar Rapids.

To build anticipation for our movie showing and meet the needs of our families, we decided to hold activities on early release Wednesdays, followed by in-house showings of the various MCU movies. The activities on Wednesdays included crafts, slime, STEAM activities, obstacle courses, trivia, mystery-solving, and a costume contest. Some programs even tempted Roblox devotees off their computers!

The final program, the showing of *Avengers: Endgame*, was at Marcus Theaters, and they were wonderful to work with all along the way. In the end, we sold 127 tickets out of 128 seats in the theater. Two library staff members arrived about an hour before the movie started, and theater staff had a few tables set up and our pre-purchased concessions ready to go. Despite a minor seating issue, everything went incredibly smoothly, and everyone enjoyed the show!

In total, the entire program series had over 500 attendees to our 20 movies and 13 programs. Our best attended in-house movie, by far, was the showing of *Avengers: Infinity War* the night before we went to *Avengers: Endgame*. The Superhero Costume Contest had the highest attendance of our other activities, with Superhero Slime a close second.

Overall, we were very pleased with the end result. Our director was even approached by one of our sponsors six months later, asking when our next themed program series would be!

Once we had started planning our "What a Marvel-ous Spring" program series, it quickly became apparent that it would be similar in scale to a summer reading program. Therefore, a fundraising effort of the same size was required. The first item of business was, of course, to figure out exactly how much money we needed to raise. Marcus Theaters quickly gave us the cost for booking an auditorium, and from there we developed a budget for the other activities, including supplies, prizes, and food.

To make sure we weren't overburdening our usual summer sponsors, we made a list of businesses and organizations we had never asked before. A few regular donors still made the list, but only the ones who are always interested in sponsoring library programs. We also researched local franchised businesses for grant opportunities. It was a delight to discover that the city's utility providers had grants available for children's programs. Our list of prospective donors included twenty-two businesses and organizations, including banks, insurance agents, realtors, dentists, law offices, a florist, a car dealership, the veterinary clinic, and the local hospital. Although the list could have included more, we limited ourselves so we wouldn't be overwhelmed.

In order to further lighten the load, the list was split in half. Our director took the half which included the largest asks, those for the banks and the Friends of the Library, and our youth services librarian took the other half. Each business was first called, to request an in-person meeting. We felt in-person meetings were important because we felt that our enthusiasm would be infectious. Several of the businesses refused the in-person meeting, requesting the information be e-mailed to them. None of these businesses elected to sponsor the program.

Our meetings with the potential sponsors were straightforward. If they didn't know anything about the Marvel movies, we briefly filled them in and then explained what the program series would entail. Finally, we told them how they could help. It wasn't just money we asked for! They were given the option of donating swag for prizes and even donating their time to help. We left each potential sponsor with a formal request letter, a form (with suggested amounts of $25, $50, $75, or $100) to send in with their donation, and a draft program brochure.

We ultimately raised $950 from sponsors to cover the in-house movie showings, supplies for activities, prizes, and advertisements. The *Avengers: Endgame* showing was the most expensive single program we have ever done, with a total cost of $1,505. However, with the three local banks pitching in $585 and our Friends of the Library giving $285, our 127 attendees only had to pay $5 for each ticket to cover the remaining $635. There was some worry that the $5 fee might still be a barrier for some patrons. Individual community members blew us away by pre-paying for tickets to give away to anyone who would find $5 a hardship. It's always incredible how generous people can be to others!

Our final tally didn't quite fit into the "little budget" category, at least for us. In fact, this program series cost about as much as all of our other programs combined for that year. But after the huge success of our fundraising efforts, we allowed ourselves to dream big and created a "marvel-ous" experience for our community.

Baked Potato Bar Fundraiser

CHELSEA PRICE, Meservey Public Library, Meservey, Iowa

We have small fundraisers here and there throughout the year, but our big one—our signature fundraiser—is our baked potato bar. It is always held on the last Wednesday in February, so people have come to look forward to and expect it. It has increased in attendance and in the funds raised each year we've held it, and we always receive very positive feedback. The potatoes, cheese, and ham are usually donated by our local bar, our board members and volunteers bake cookies, and the library purchases the drinks and a few other toppings. I also set up a small book and movie sale. Since we don't have the space for a large event, the town fire station lets us use their building. We ask for a free-will donation rather than a specific fee—I have found that asking for a donation of any amount actually tends to bring in more money in the end. The first year, we raised around $800; the most recent year, we raised almost $1,200! The money goes toward our annual summer carnival.

This event seems to do a lot as far as community-building is concerned. People from all different walks of life gather together, eat a hot meal, talk, and laugh—it's a wonderful thing to see. Last year, we had people from towns as far as thirty minutes away! We always see and talk to people we've never met before, and they're always extremely complimentary about what our library is doing. This just goes to show that you never know who is watching from afar and has noticed all the awesome things your library is offering!

GET THOSE GRANTS

Even though signature fundraising events can be a lot of fun, they can also be a lot of work for just a small amount of money. Sometimes libraries need a *large* chunk of money in a short amount of time, and they don't have the time to plan a big event. That's where grants come in. Grant applications and proposals can seem intimidating—there's usually lots of detailed questions involved, and many librarians are worried that their writing won't be good enough to create a persuasive proposal. Plus, there are so many community organizations in need who are also applying; how on earth can you make your proposal stand out from the competition? Well, worry not! Anyone (yes, anyone!) has the ability to write a grant, and though it can be tough at first, you'll pick up some skills and tricks as you go, and it gets much easier once you've written and received that first grant.

Choose your project wisely. First, always keep an "ideas folder," a place where your library keeps information related to projects that it would like to eventually complete. Grant applications can crop up quickly, so it's nice to have some detailed ideas handy in case your due date comes up sooner than you think. The best projects will be unique and stand out from the crowd. If you know that a nearby library or organization is applying for the same grant for the exact same project you're trying for, think about sending in an application for that particular project somewhere else. You don't want your application to be identical to that of another organization. In general, funders tend to choose projects that meet a need in the community, offer something innovative and out-of-the-box, and have measurable outcomes that can be replicated and are sustainable. And you get bonus points if your project includes community involvement and partnerships! More than money, grants are about impact, and you want to make it clear that your project will have a positive impact in the community.

Follow directions. The ability to follow instructions is absolutely necessary when it comes to receiving grants. You need to make sure that you're giving the foundation all of the information that they need to make a decision. If an applicant fails to follow instructions, chances are that the application will be thrown out immediately. Most agencies will not take the time to reach out to an individual applicant to ask for more information. Be careful to check and double-check your work, fixing any spelling or grammatical errors, and remember not to use abbreviations or lingo that nonlibrarians wouldn't understand—"ILL" or "makerspace" might not mean much to the person reading your application.

Think community over library. When applying for a grant, think beyond just your library. Think about how your project will affect or improve not just the library, but the community as a whole. If a foundation can see that the impact of a project will go much further than the library's walls, they will be more likely to fund it.

Don't sell your library short. Even though your library may be desperately in need of more funding, don't make that too obvious in a grant proposal. Agencies want to feel sure that your library is capable enough to continue this project and make it work even after the grant money runs out. Point out your library's strengths rather than just your needs—you want your funder to believe that you are worthy of investing and believing in. Talk about previous successes you have had with similar projects, and discuss how you will have adequate resources to continue doing awesome things in the future. Your funders don't want to feel like they are your library's only hope for success, and that you're destitute and dependent on only them for a project (even if you feel like that's true, just keep it to yourself!). Think of it like this: your library is awesome, and with their help, it could be even *awesomer!* (But don't use "awesomer"; that's not a real word.)

Be passionate, but don't ramble. Don't be afraid to brag a little about your library. If you feel passionately about the project, make that clear in your proposal. Funders want to know that you truly care about what they're putting money toward. Include not only numbers and statistics, but also heartwarming or poignant anecdotes about your library or the project. If you're looking to get a Lego Club funded, talk about that shy young patron who you had never heard speak before he started bonding with other kids over Legos. Mention that dad who has regularly scheduled supervised visitations with his daughter at your library, and the thing that seems to help them communicate is building things with Legos together. Make your funder feel something. If there is emotion connected to what they're reading, it will stick with them and make your application more memorable. Capturing readers' hearts means that your proposal is interesting and engaging. However, be careful that you aren't rambling—there's a difference between being passionate and just being long-winded.

Reach out. If you're unsure about your proposal, and are worried that it's boring or doesn't make sense, find someone who is willing to read it and give you their honest feedback. The best person is probably another librarian or someone who has written (and received) multiple grants themselves. They know what to look for and will be able to help and guide you.

Collect data. If you're successful, don't forget to follow up with your funders, filling out all the necessary evaluation forms and including all the data they need. They want to know exactly what their money has gone toward and how it has impacted the library and community. Include a few photos to show the project in action.

IT'S NOT OVER YET!

Once you have received a grant, gift, or donation, you might think that all you have left to do is spend the money. Wrong! There's more work still to be done, even after the money is spent. Not only do you need to fill out your grant report and make sure you've completed all of the follow-up questions required by your funder, but you also need to complete a few easy but important tasks in order to really solidify and maintain that relationship between the donor and your library.

Start with a simple thank-you note, sent promptly after you receive the gift, grant, or donation. Saying thank you really does matter, and a handwritten letter to express your appreciation is a necessity with any donation or gift, no matter how small. If you don't have the time to personally write out each note yourself, try to find a volunteer or staff member who's willing to do it. The small touches can often make the biggest difference, and that thank-you note might be the difference between getting the grant again next year and never receiving one again. Everyone likes to feel appreciated, including your funders!

Try to keep in touch with your donors throughout the year. Include them in library e-mail newsletters, send them photos of patrons enjoying whatever their donation helped pay for (along with some positive feedback from the community), and drop them a card during the holidays. This helps them remember your library, possibly cultivating future gifts.

The donor should be thanked not only personally, but also publicly—on your website, social media pages, and local news media. Send an article to your local newspaper with a photo of the funded project, letting both the community and the funder know how excited people are about your new programs. If the donor has helped fund a specific program, make sure you acknowledge that on all the advertising you do for that program—and if the donor is a business, include their logo on your flyers.

At the end of your fiscal year, why not throw a little donor appreciation event? Invite the entire community, including all donors and city council members. Serve some snacks and coffee, play some music, and show some gratitude to your generous donors. Some libraries even have a donor wall with plaques or decorations featuring individual donors' names; others feature a different donor each month on their Facebook page.

If you *weren't* funded and didn't get that grant you were hoping for, don't give up! Ask for the grant reviewers' feedback, so you can get an idea of whether you did something wrong, or they just didn't have enough money to fund your project this time around. Then you can try again next year, or edit and revise the application and try getting a grant from another source. Don't lose faith—just because one foundation didn't want to fund you doesn't mean another won't!

10

Extra, Extra, Read All About It

NOW THAT YOU'VE READ ABOUT VARIOUS PROGRAM IDEAS AND how to fund them, the only thing left to do is to actually get people to attend—and that's a pretty important step! It's time to bring your excited patrons to your programs in droves, make good use of those extra snacks and craft supplies, and impress your board with your off-the-charts attendance numbers! But how? How do you get butts in seats at your events? The answer is *marketing*.

Most librarians aren't trained in marketing at all, but you don't have to get another degree to market your library successfully. If you're not lucky enough to have a marketing or PR department at your library, you'll have to take it on yourself . . . and it's totally worth the effort! Great marketing can make the difference between a program where you have rock star–level crowds and a program that results in a room full of empty chairs.

If you've had a program flop before and you just can't figure out the reason, there is a chance that your marketing wasn't quite effective enough. You can have an amazing event in the works, but if you don't have a great strategy in place for spreading the word about it, all of the time you spent planning and setting it up could be for nothing. Libraries with already small budgets tend to balk at the idea of putting time, money, and effort into spreading the word about their services, but it's something that must be done if you want to have people at your programs. Read on to learn about various methods of marketing and how to use them successfully at your library!

HAVE YOU HEARD?

Before social media and TV advertisements, word of mouth was the original form of marketing. Word-of-mouth marketing has power——most people are more likely to listen to their friends or family than they are to an ad on Facebook or in the newspaper. If a person is impressed with your library's services, they're probably going to tell someone . . . and then that person might tell someone else . . . and so on, until your library's actions have gone, in a sense, viral. One of the best ways to start a word-of-mouth marketing wildfire is to constantly be a library advocate.

Advocacy is often thought of as lobbying or rallying for a political cause, but there's much more to it than that. Being a library advocate can be as simple as talking up your library—brag about what you offer to the community, discuss the value of the library, and the changes you're making in your town. You know the many ways in which a library can change a life . . . make sure that everyone else knows it, too! Of course you're an advocate when you're leading programs, bringing storytimes to day care centers, and asking donors to help with library funding, but what about when you're just behind the circulation desk? What about when you're out in the community for nonlibrary reasons?

Advocacy is especially important in small towns where everyone knows who you are. That's one of the nice things about being a "public figure" in a small area. Communities often know your name, who your parents are, where you live, and how many dogs you have. When you go into the bank, one of your former teachers is the teller. Your old high school friend brings her kids to all your programs. Some people probably even knew you when you were little, and visiting the library yourself. There's a great sense of belonging and neighborly kindness when you grow up and work in a small town. You feel like you belong. Patrons typically trust you and support the things you do.

However, the downside of this is that *everyone knows who you are.* When you're out and about in your town, someone sees you and immediately associates you with the library. When you're at lunch, visiting the post office, or going for a walk, chances are that you'll run into a patron or supporter of your library. Gossip is prevalent in towns like these, and if you are seen doing something that may be perceived negatively, people will start spreading the word, and it will reflect back on your library. If you're a director in a small-town library, it's important to remember that you are the face of the library, and you should act accordingly when you attend nonlibrary events.

It can be difficult to keep that smile on your face and pretend you're Pollyanna when you're in the public eye, but it is important. This doesn't mean that you can't be yourself—of course not. But it does mean you'll need to be a lot more conscious of yourself, your behavior, and even what you post on social media. When you attend a fundraiser for a local church or grab a bite at the town watering hole, be aware that someone is most likely paying attention. Even when you're "off," you still have to be "on," in a sense—the library is a reflection of *you*. Remember that infectious energy you read about in the outreach chapter? Try to maintain that as best you can when you're out at community events. If you're positive, friendly, and passionate about your job, word-of-mouth marketing will happen on its own simply because you're so enjoyable to be around.

When you're in the library working the desk, you should never keep quiet about the awesome programs you have in store. If you can't or don't want to hand out brochures or flyers to every patron who comes in, just mention upcoming programs casually. With each patron interaction, find ways to bring up programs or exciting new additions. "I'm sorry it's such a mess in here; we're preparing for a _____ program on Friday!" This will probably receive a follow-up question about the event, and it also gives you a great excuse for your messy library! You would be surprised how many people look right through all those flyers you've got hung up and don't even know what you have going on. Also, if your other staff members, trustees, family, and friends aren't already making attempts to be library advocates, encourage them to share social media posts, mention your programs when libraries come up in conversation, and basically just talk the library up when they get the chance.

Being an advocate doesn't necessarily mean you're constantly pitching your services to your friends and family. "Have you heard we now offer Kanopy streaming services at our library?" is an awfully random thing to just put out there during a family dinner, and they will probably get annoyed with you after a while. But if you're excited about a new program series that you recently spearheaded, bring it up! If you got amazing feedback or a funny comment about a new addition to your children's area, brag a little! It's totally possible to talk about your library without directly promoting something and sounding like a door-to-door salesman; tell a story instead, share an anecdote. Librarians are often too humble and hesitant to toot their own horn, and your humility is holding you back—go ahead! Do some tootin'!

Another large part of advocacy is to become "embedded" in your community. Don't let your community associate you *only* with the library building. Get out there, go where your town is, and thrust yourself into becoming an active, involved member of the community. While outreach is a necessary part of being a librarian, it's not exactly the same as being embedded; outreach is occasionally going out into the community to promote a service, while embedded librarianship is consistently being integrated in your community.

Join a club, attend nonlibrary events, and hang out where others like to hang out. Being embedded allows you to really get to know your community, which helps you serve them better. It also allows your community to get to know you as an individual rather than just a librarian. You want to establish trust with the people of your community and make them feel comfortable around you.

THEY "LIKE" US, THEY REALLY "LIKE" US!

Word-of-mouth marketing has largely moved to an Internet-based platform, with reviews, rants, and raves about all kinds of businesses and organizations all over social media. People recommend things online now more than they do in person, and they can share your content and events with just the click of a button. This makes word-of-mouth marketing for your library quicker and more efficient, but it can be complex too. How do you deal with a negative Facebook review? What can you do to get more interaction on social media? How do I reach a larger audience if they don't "like" my library's page?

Many businesses and organizations seem to be focused more on collecting "likes" than on interacting with their followers on social media. They get caught up in the numbers and forget that a social media page should be all about engaging with customers and patrons. But the truth is, just because someone "likes" us on Facebook doesn't mean they're connecting with us, checking out materials, and attending events. Having one million followers on social media doesn't mean anything if they're not sharing, commenting, and interacting with you on a daily basis. It's much more effective to have just 100 followers who are connected, engaged, and advocating for your library.

These days, fewer people have newspaper subscriptions than they used to. And we can't rely on radio or TV advertisements to reach everyone, since many people stream their music and TV shows nowadays. While we should still use those other outlets when necessary, social media seems to be the way to go when it comes to reaching a majority of the population.

While Pinterest has somewhat fallen out of favor lately, it is still a popular site for creating inspiration boards, and libraries can use it to advertise new materials, show off library displays and programs, create readers' advisory boards, and curate helpful learning materials for parents. Twitter is great for quotes and bite-sized pieces of information, while Instagram is used solely for eye-catching photos and short videos. Teens have migrated toward SnapChat and TikTok, and YouTube is still quite popular for longer video content—but teens don't seem to be on Facebook anymore at all. (If you want to reach the teen age group, your library *definitely* has to be using social media.) The majority of libraries, though, seem to have settled on Facebook as the best way to connect with parents, families, and older adults, as well as the community as a whole by using group pages.

One of the nice things about Facebook is the ability to join many different groups. If there's a group for your town, school district, or local clubs . . . get in there and start interacting! You also have the ability to create events and invite people to them (although that definitely doesn't mean that if 25 people click "interested," 25 people will show up!), as well as invite people to "like" your page. Facebook also allows you to schedule posts for busier times—7:00 a.m. and 5:00 p.m. tend to be the most active times to post something. You can "pin" big events or important news to the top of your page so it's the first thing your followers will see, which can be helpful. Another fun feature Facebook includes is the ability to track insights and keep an eye on what kinds of posts people are engaging with the most; this helps you create a social media marketing plan.

Facebook Ads, while they do cost money, can be quite effective. Libraries with no money to spend on advertising may not find it worth their while, but paying for an ad to run for a short time on Facebook can bring in a lot of new likes and attendees. If you're having a large program and want lots of attendance, Facebook Ads is something to consider. It allows you to target your audience, so if your event is for children, you can target younger adults to get the attention of parents. If your ad is for a book club, you can widen that audience to be directed at young adults all the way through seniors. You end up getting a great bang for your buck, and you reach far more people than you would have without using the function.

As soon as your library ventures into a new social media platform, you should follow not only other organizations, groups, and businesses in your area, but also other libraries that you admire and would love to emulate. Libraries all over the world are doing amazing things, and by following your "competitors" on social media, you can pick up some great ideas and learn from your fellow librarians.

Social media allows libraries to reach people of all ages for free—by creating fun, engaging posts, you become content-providers. When libraries use social media in a creative way, they can even engage patrons with passive programs that are completely online, like a photography contest or a social media book club. Some of these online passive programs can even be reported as participation in your end-of-year reports.

SOCIAL MEDIA BEST PRACTICES

Include video content. People love short (60 seconds or less) videos! Whether it's a slow-motion video of your staff breaking in the new storytime parachute or a cat pawing at the library doors, your followers will eat it up. Do a skit with your coworker, or create a parody movie trailer about the library. Make a music video promoting summer reading, and do brief video booktalks on new releases. Near Thanksgiving, have patrons fill out a sign that says "I'm thankful for libraries because _____" and then create a video of them holding the signs set to music. When using social media, it's important to show rather than tell, so don't just talk about your update of the children's area; *show* your followers the new additions using video. Wear a costume, add music, and *have fun!* If you're the subject of the video, loosen up and pretend you're having a conversation with a friend, and remember that it's supposed to be fun and casual. And when in doubt, a video featuring a cute dog or cat is always a hit!

Tell a story. There are many different kinds of stories you can share on your library's social media, and who doesn't love a great story? Talk about how the library impacted someone, how that person's life changed because of the library (with their permission, of course). Tell your followers about a recent donation that made the new computers possible, or talk about your community and the different ways it supports the library. Tell a story about your staff members or patrons. Share that cute thing that happened at storytime yesterday that will make people say "Awwww!" Don't be afraid to get personal if you'd like, though not too often—sharing a brief anecdote about how a librarian changed your life as a child can be very impactful. Keep it short and sweet, and try to make readers feel something. Stories and emotions can often make a much bigger difference to followers than facts and information.

Be positive and deal with negativity properly. While libraries' social media pages are often very positive spaces, there is always that chance that someone will post a negative (and sometimes nasty) comment or review. If this happens to you, don't panic. Be respectful toward the negative feedback if it is constructive, and respond calmly rather than defensively. Offer an apology and validate the person's feelings, and then offer a solution—see if they need to speak to someone besides you, and then make that happen. Be authentic and genuine. If the negativity continues, take it offline and message them personally. If this person's negative comment is not constructive in any way—whether it's a personal attack, a derogatory comment, or includes slurs or foul language—you may just want to delete their comment. Trolls are all over the Internet, and it's best not to feed them.

If you are running your library's social media accounts, it's your job to create a safe and supportive space online where your followers feel comfortable and enjoy interacting. You should avoid posting anything that takes a political or religious stance, and try to avoid anything that will start a controversy on the page. If you're in doubt about a post, just don't post it! Your library's social media page is not the place to complain, argue, or talk poorly about anyone. Keep it upbeat, positive, and professional.

Don't shy away from humor. Humor is often what makes one library's social media account stand out from the others. If you're up-to-date on current memes, join in on the fun! Make a meme of your own that pertains to libraries, or re-create the meme in a photo. Try to stay current and relevant—don't post about something that happened months ago. Include a variety of entertaining content, including funny quotes about reading or libraries, listicles or quizzes, and clever captions to your photos. Many libraries acknowledge holidays in clever ways, such as advertising a Black Friday sale in the stacks—"100% off everything in-store and online!" The best library-run social media pages are current, topical, creative, and humorous!

Be consistent. It can be stressful to try and figure out what to post and when to post it. This is where an editorial calendar can be very helpful. If you stay ahead of the game and write down your content ideas a month beforehand, you'll be living on Easy Street when it comes to your social media content. The scheduling tool on Facebook can also be helpful in this regard. You want to post often, but not *too* often—once daily is usually a good rule. Stay consistent by trying to post around the same time each day. You also want to always try and respond quickly to any comments or messages you get.

Don't be self-centered. Even though the center of attention on a library's social media page will of course be the library itself, it's important not to put the focus *only* on the library. The general rule of thumb is that only 30 percent of your posts should be actively promoting something at the library; the other 70 percent should be more engaging posts. The engaging posts can vary wildly. You can ask people what they're reading, offer live reader's advisory, post historical photos of the community, share book-related products, create a library-related chart or infographic, find little-known facts about popular books or authors, talk about what's going on in your community, or share local non-library events. Just because the majority of your posts shouldn't be promotional doesn't mean they can't also pertain to your library—post a behind-the-scenes photo of your staff trying to clean up after a wild storytime, or a funny title you came across when weeding books, by all means. They just shouldn't all be promotional, that's all.

Steal These Ideas!

Use popular hashtags. Hashtags are an easier way to search for and follow specific words or phrases on Facebook, Instagram, and Twitter. If someone is interested in a specific topic, they can search for the hashtag and find a bunch of posts relevant to what they were looking for. A super-popular one is #tbt (Throwback Thursday), when social media users post an old "throwback" photo.

Promote unusual holidays. Check out the National Day Calendar website to find the most random and unusual holidays, then celebrate them on your social media pages. There's National Donut Day (first Friday in June *or* November 5), National Dog Day (August 26), National Random Acts of

Kindness Day (February 17), and so much more! You could also celebrate themed months like No Shave November, National Bike Month (May), and LGBT Pride Month (June). All of these would make for some amazing and engaging social media posts!

Start a Kindness Rocks campaign. The rock-painting craze that hit the streets in 2015 is still going strong today. Many libraries have done rock-painting programs, then hid the rocks painted with words of encouragement all around their town. When someone stumbled across one, they would post a photo to the library's social media. It's a heartwarming activity that also creates great photos to post on various social media platforms.

Take polls. Social media polls are similar to the whiteboard polls we talked about in the section on passive programming, and they can be both fun *and* helpful. Ask fun questions as an engaging post, or ask your followers' opinion on something. What Hogwarts House are your followers in? Would your followers rather come to book club on Wednesday or Thursday evenings? The possibilities with polls are truly endless.

Do some reader's advisory. If you have a quiet night ahead of you, consider hopping on social media to do some reader's advisory with your followers. Post something like "Find your next favorite book! Comment your most recent favorite read, and I'll recommend another for you to try next!" Give commenters a book suggestion based on the genre of book they like, and if you aren't sure what to recommend . . . just head over to Google!

Host live trivia. This can be done in a similar way to the reader's advisory, except with trivia questions instead of book recommendations. If you're feeling brave, you can also use the Facebook or Instagram Live function and talk in real time to your followers.

Highlight milestones. Is there an important library anniversary coming up? Is it your library assistant's or favorite patron's birthday? Will someone be retiring soon? Make a post about it! Your followers love knowing what's going on at the library and in the community.

Tag authors. If you take a photo or create a post about a specific book or series of books, tag the author on Instagram and Twitter! Some authors love to interact with fans on social media, and it will be a fun surprise for your followers when Stephen King comments on your post about his new brick of a novel. (He probably won't. But you could still try!)

Post videos of book dominoes. Grab a bunch of books that are all roughly the same size, then stand them up in a row to create dominoes. Create crazy, intricate patterns all throughout the library, then knock 'em over and take a video of it! If you have a page or a shelver, they're probably going to be mad at you. And if you're a one-person library and you have to pick all those books up yourself, I'm sorry. But do it for the 'Gram!

Share your Day in the Life. If you have time, take a day to show your social media followers how exactly you spend your day. Headed to a park to do an outreach storytime? Take a photo on the way. Working on next year's budget? Take a slow-motion video of you tossing crumpled papers in the air while looking miserable. (This kind of post—posting frequently throughout one day—might be best suited for Instagram Stories, where your followers can scroll through pictures and videos quickly, and the content disappears after twenty-four hours.) Followers will love seeing just exactly what it is you do every day—contrary to popular belief, you aren't just reading the day away behind a desk!

Feature patrons or staff. Each week or month, choose a different patron or staff member to spotlight on your social media page. Take a photo—with permission, don't be a creep!—and come up with a few sentences about them and what the library means to them. Your community will love seeing familiar faces and learning more about the people in town!

Post about anything involving animals. When in doubt, post a photo or video of an animal. Any animal. Doing anything, really. I promise you it will have more "likes" than your previous three posts put together.

7 Places to Advertise

Figure out where your target audience is, then advertise there. Don't limit your advertising to inside the library—many people who might like to attend your program aren't library users at all—and always ask permission first.

1. **Bathrooms**—Hang flyers on the inside of the stall, not only at your library, but at other places too!

2. **Schools**—Whether you hang flyers in the teachers' lounge, office bulletin boards, or ask teachers to send them home with kids, schools are the perfect place to advertise. If you can swing it, get an advertisement in the yearbook, in sports event programs, and on the morning announcements.

3. **Senior centers**—You could advertise for all kinds of adult programs at a senior center: book club, crafting program, exercise group, and more!

4. **Local businesses**—Gas stations, boutiques, restaurants, Starbucks, the list goes on. Don't count out other nonprofit organizations like animal shelters, churches, and youth centers.

5. **Grocery store**—Many grocery stores have bulletin boards that they might let you advertise on.

6. **Post office**—If your town is small, maybe surrounding towns' post offices will let you advertise there too.

7. **Bank**—There's almost always a community bulletin board at the bank.

WAYS TO ADVERTISE

Aside from hanging flyers, here are some more ways to advertise your library programs in effective ways. Some methods are tried-and-true, while others are a little more out-of-the-box, but all of them are doable for all kinds of libraries!

Steal These Ideas!

Create e-mail notifications or e-mail signatures. E-mail is not often used to advertise in smaller libraries, but it's a sure way to reach your patrons. You can also include program or library information in your automated e-mail signature so that it's included in every e-mail you send out.

Write and send a press release. Contact local media and put together a brief press release about an upcoming program.

Submit announcements to local church bulletins. Find out who is responsible for typing up the local church bulletins, then reach out to them to see if you could add a few lines.

Submit news to be included with the water bill. Some small towns will allow their library to include a half-page of news or advertising with the water bill.

Invest in sidewalk signs and chalk. Sidewalk signs are effective during programs to draw people in, while chalking sidewalks is often used on college campuses to alert students to events.

We added balloons to our sidewalk sign for our Elizabeth Berg program.

Create eye-catching window or book displays. Include program information along with your window and book displays.

Slip bookmarks inside library books. Type up and print out some customized bookmarks, then hide them inside popular books.

Design some wearable ads. Wear an advertisement on your body, whether it's a customized T-shirt, lanyard, button, or pin—it's sure to get a lot of questions!

Submit news to community event calendars. Whether it's for your county or your town, e-mail the people who put the community events calendar together to make sure the library is included.

Write a library newsletter (print or online). Try creating a brief, monthly newsletter for your library. Offer it up in print or online using a service like Mailchimp.

Send announcements through direct mail. This is probably a strategy that is used most often in very small towns, where it is possible to reach the majority of your town through the mail without breaking the bank.

Design some bar coasters. Create customized coasters through VistaPrint and ask your local bar if they will use them or give them out.

Create some magnets. Order customized magnets at a reasonable price through VistaPrint and give them not only to patrons, but also to local businesses to hang wherever they can.

Inquire about submitting a movie theater ad. At small theaters, there are often ads for local businesses before the movie starts.

Inquire about doing a radio ad. Most local radio stations are willing to give some airtime to promote various community events.

Create a receipt printer message. If your library gives out receipts at checkout, take advantage of that advertising space!

Design a library computer screensaver. All of the *Fortnite*-playing kids and teens will have to look at your advertisement on their screensaver!

Utilize TV screens or digital picture frames at the library desk. People are more likely to pay attention to a scrolling screen of programs than to a printed flyer.

Put messages on a billboard or marquee sign. If you're lucky enough to have one!

THINGS TO CONSIDER

Examine your space through a patron's eyes. Walk through your library building with clear eyes as if you are a patron. Are things easy to reach? Is everything clearly labeled? Can you find each section without needing help? (I mean, of course *you* can, but can your patrons?) Do you have the Dewey Decimal system still in place in your nonfiction sections? That's fine, as long as your patrons have no trouble finding what they're looking for, but if they're having trouble, should you consider switching to shelving by category instead? Merchandising is a big part of marketing, and you want your space to be inclusive, easy to navigate, and pleasing to the eye. (This goes for your library website, too—if it's not easy to navigate, it needs to be updated.) If your reading areas don't make you want to cuddle up with a book, do something about it! If your children's section doesn't make kids shriek in excitement, change something! Create spaces in your building that feel like little neighborhoods—this will make your patrons feel at home, and they'll be likelier to spend more time there.

Create a blog or a podcast. Library blogs have been around for quite some time, but they're just as popular as ever. If you have the time to keep it updated, having a library blog is a great way to advertise programs, as well as report on how programs went and give patrons a behind-the-scenes look at your job. In the same vein, library podcasts are very popular, though they're a bit more difficult to start than a blog. People love podcasts because they can listen to them in the car, on a run, while doing laundry, whenever! There are a few super-popular library podcasts out there, including Two Librarians and a Microphone and The Librarian Is In, but there's a noticeable lack of small/rural library podcasts out there . . . so start one!

Market your brand. Your library should have a brand. A brand is more than just a tagline or logo (though you should have those things too!); it is the feeling people have when they think about your library. What feeling do you want to evoke in your patrons? Comfort? Joy? Nostalgia? Pick one of those and stick with it whenever you advertise. When you market your library creatively, you have the ability to completely shift your community's viewpoint about the library and libraries in general. Lots of people still have very outdated views of the library—they believe they will be shushed if they so much as cough. Marketing your library differently can change this! Libraries are increasingly being seen as fun, diverse, inclusive, innovative, and modern, and this is in large part due to marketing.

Get a brand mascot. Having a mascot can further your brand—it doesn't have to be a live animal, but if you are able to have a library pet, then go for it! It can also be a puppet, stuffed animal, or even just a picture or cartoon. Whatever it is, if the community responds well to it, be consistent—post about your mascot on social media, give it a name, put pictures of it on flyers. A mascot can reinvigorate patrons' interest in your library and draw in new ones, and it makes your library seem more fun and playful.

Market big programs in a big way. You can't market your weekly book club in the same way that you market your annual carnival fundraiser. The bigger the program, the bigger your marketing strategy has to be. If you've got a *huge* event coming up that you need great attendance at, contact *everyone*—schools, radio stations, TV news, newspapers, businesses, patrons, family, friends, everyone. If you're partnering with various businesses or organizations, ask them to advertise the event as well. You can even ask other local libraries to help you—we've gotta support our own! You won't need to take these steps for a smaller program like an after-school club or storytime. Not every program will be advertised in the same way, or on the same scale.

Give out swag. Everyone loves free stuff—candy, pens, notebooks, stickers—and if it's got your library's name and logo emblazoned on it, then your patrons will be doing your advertising for you! The use of swag is about more than just giving away fun items, though. It increases the awareness of your library, it's a conversation-starter, and it creates a positive memory of the library in your patrons' minds—every time they pick up that color-changing pencil, they'll think of the library!

Provide stellar service. You will always need to advertise in some way, but if you provide exceptional service and offer small, personal touches, the chances are that people already love your library. That's why it's so important that you stay upbeat and friendly, and try to get to know your patrons, at least well enough to greet them by name. Think your programs through and try to cater to the community's wants and needs, and offer a warm and inviting atmosphere—all the marketing in the world won't help much if you don't have those basics already down pat.

IDEAS IN ACTION

Libraries Are for Everyone Campaign

REBECCA MCCORKINDALE, Gretna Public Library, Gretna, Nebraska

I recently attended a joint library association conference between Iowa and Nebraska, and I was thrilled that the two marketing sessions were standing-room only. (I actually had to sit on the floor during one of them.) But this was the first time I had seen such eagerness about acquiring marketing skills, and it gives me hope that libraries everywhere are wising up to how very important marketing is to their existence.

I spent almost a decade prior to entering the library world learning about marketing, and eventually I became the head of marketing in a midwestern district for a large bookstore chain. It was because of this experience that I immediately saw how far behind many libraries (our own included) were in terms of marketing themselves. And we desperately need to get into the marketing game in order to help advocate for their existence.

Something that I learned over time in the library world is that there should be a "voice" for your marketing. Let's take social media posts. I would look for the funniest book or library-related memes or images to share, which was very much in keeping with my personality. But is that what I want people to associate with our library? Not always. When we stepped back and analyzed the feel of what I was posting, it veered too much into comedy. What we wanted instead was to convey an open, welcoming, and intelligent presence.

The whole point of marketing is to get people through your doors. It's usually the first impression anyone gets about your library. Imagine a patron who has just moved to your town, and they decide to check out the library. What do most people do nowadays? They look up the library's website online. How user-friendly is it? Is the basic information easy to find? Are the images fresh and in touch with the modern world? How is your logo—do you even *have* a logo? Is your website doing everything possible to convey a sense of welcome to anyone who visits it? This alone will either draw a potential patron in or scare them away.

And the most important thing is to realize that everyone on your library team is a marketer for your library: how they interact with patrons, if they create flyers or displays—this is all part of marketing. You should really embrace the idea that marketing is a team effort, and have as many staff as possible pursue some continuing education in this field.

The best example of teamwork marketing was our creation of the Libraries Are for Everyone campaign (aka LAFE). Many people think of me immediately when these signs are posted, but the campaign would never have happened without two other library workers reaching out to me. I had been upset that the summer artwork in the Collaborative Summer Library Program kit only represented us disabled people as being in wheelchairs. I channeled my angry energy into creating alternative artwork that could supplement libraries' art choices, where I tried to show the diversity that normally isn't represented in marketing materials.

A few months later Julie Syler, the innovations librarian at the Saline County Library in Arkansas, reached out to me. She was working on the marketing for her state's library advocacy day. She wanted input or help on her creation which used my alternative art. I took one look at the poster she sent me and I knew, without a doubt, what these signs needed to look like—she was sooo close to nailing it, and it just took someone with a bit more marketing and design savvy to "tweak" the poster to what she had hoped it would be.

That story would have been a great ending right there, but then it continued. Ludy Rueda, a member of the Poudre River Public Library District's Bilingual and Multicultural Outreach Services, e-mailed me. It was a lovely e-mail where she thanked me for the signs, and as part of her sign-off, she shared the Spanish translation of "Libraries Are for Everyone." Her simple e-mail was the creative spark that made me realize how the LAFE campaign could be so much more than just seven different signs in English. And thus began the LAFE campaign which everyone in the library world knows about, and which will be hitting over 100 translations of its message in the upcoming months.

What I hope you take away from this origin story is that you never know what impact your marketing skills could have, either to your community or to the whole world. I changed the focus of my blog *Hafuboti* after I realized that it would be a great way to share the marketing and creativity of my library team and myself.

If you haven't checked out or downloaded any of the LAFE signs, then you really should! Visit Hafuboti.com and look on the right-hand side for the tags. You can't miss the large "Libraries Are for Everyone" link. Even better? E-mail me with a new translation, but be sure to check out the "LAFE Library" on my blog first in order to see if that translation has already been posted. I am thrilled whenever a librarian reaches out to show me how they've used my signs, and I'm always even *more* thrilled that someone has chosen to use some of my work to help market to their community what a library is.

Ultimately, if you're marketing effectively, then you don't have to work as hard to justify your existence to your community and your local government. Tap into the fact that the public library can be the greatest PR tool for local government to have. And marketing shouldn't be a scary thing—it should be something done in increments. Learn some marketing basics, and begin brainstorming how you could implement these principles in your library. Once you start gaining some knowledge and skills, marketing should become easier and more exciting. You never know—your work could gain worldwide notice.

FIGURE 10.1 / Libraries Are for Everyone

11

Take This Job and . . . Love It!

WORKING IN A SMALL OR RURAL LIBRARY CAN BE A TOUGH GIG. You might be set apart geographically from other libraries, which can feel incredibly isolating, and even more so if you're a one-person show with no staff to lean on. You often have little or no budget to work with when it comes to programming, and maybe you're scraping the bottom of the barrel when it comes to new, creative ideas that won't cost the library anything. Maybe you feel unappreciated, and all your hard work goes unnoticed, or maybe you've planned one too many programs where no one has shown up. Maybe you're juggling too many summer reading events with a too-small staff, and you just can't muster the enthusiasm.

The work you do can very easily end in job burnout, a type of work-related stress that is physically, mentally, and emotionally exhausting and can lead to some serious health issues. You've probably experienced it in some form: you no longer feel inspired or passionate about what you're doing, you lack energy, and just the thought of getting behind that circulation desk has you drained. You can't plan successful programs when you're running on empty—heck, you can barely even function in your day-to-day life! Librarians in small and rural libraries are especially susceptible to burnout, because most (if not all) of the responsibilities lie directly on their tired shoulders. Does this resonate with

4 Key Symptoms of Burnout

1. **Irritability or cynicism.** If you find yourself losing your temper with the Roblox-obsessed kids squabbling over the computer or inwardly criticizing everything your coworker does, take note of that feeling—you may be well on your way to burnout.

2. **Lack of energy.** If you drag yourself to work day after day and sit sluggishly behind the desk, completely unmotivated to do even the best parts of your job (toddler storytime!), that's a red flag.

3. **Dissatisfaction with accomplishments.** When things that used to make you happy just aren't doing it for you anymore, that's yet another symptom of burnout.

4. **Physical ailments.** If you're experiencing chronic stomach aches, headaches, intestinal issues, or just a feeling of overall exhaustion, those are all the calling cards of burnout. (Obviously, you should still go to the doctor to make sure there's nothing else going on—I wear a lot of hats, but "doctor" isn't one of them!)

you? Read this chapter to learn more about job burnout and what you can do to combat it.

WHAT FACTORS CONTRIBUTE TO BURNOUT?

Job expectations. Library directors in small, rural libraries are often expected to wear *all the hats all the time*. Although your degree might be in library science (or something completely unrelated), who do you think will be doing the information technology at your library? The janitorial work? The social media marketing? The outreach? The babysitting (call it whatever you like; you know it's true)? The gardening? Spoiler alert: It's you. Your library degree probably did not prepare you for the vast majority of things you're expected to do when you work in a small library, from helping a child with a bloody nose to being that certain patron's very own personal counselor. And yet, you're expected to do it all with a smile on your face. This can be a good thing, but it's a *huge* thing, as well as a whole lot of work.

Librarians in larger libraries don't have it easy either, by any means. They face other challenges, and must wear other hats: that of first responder, social worker, or advocate for the homeless, mentally ill, or drug-addicted. But in small, rural libraries you're expected to be perpetually cheerful and enthusiastic all the time, regardless of what's going on behind the scenes. Yes, communities tend to expect a whole lot from their friendly neighborhood librarians . . . but what happens when your towering stack of hats begins to wobble?

Emotional struggles related to your job. Rural librarians often end up taking on the struggles and hardships of their patrons. Since you're so ingrained in the community, you have probably formed relationships with your patrons, and you take their problems home with you—what will happen if the single mom whose resume you helped type up today can't find a job? Did that coat-less little girl who wanders into the library all alone get a nutritious meal today? Being an empathetic person can sometimes feel more like a burden than a positive quality.

Lack of job-related support. Working in a small, rural library comes with its own set of challenges. Your budgets are dwindling, yet you're expected to pump out quality programs regardless. You may be isolated from other libraries, so you're without peers to run ideas by and ask for advice. Sure, you can join an association or attend a conference where you can meet plenty of others in your position, but guess what? Those associations and conferences cost money—money you probably don't have. (The conferences also cost more for nonmembers, so you'd like to become a member to get a cheaper rate, but once again, you can't afford it.) Many state library boards don't have a representative for small or rural libraries, so you have no one who represents you, or understands your specific needs. In addition to this, it can sometimes feel that no one acknowledges, or even notices, all the good that you do for your community. Some people might genuinely believe that a librarian sits behind her desk and reads all day (if only!). This can all be disheartening, to say the least.

Chaotic work environment. Contrary to some people's belief, libraries are not the outdated, silent, "shush"-filled environments they once were. Now "shushes" are frowned upon, and the idea of the library as a community hub is more embraced than ever before. Kids are allowed—and even encouraged—to make messes, be noisy, sing, and dance. Some of your patrons may be drinking coffee and sharing gossip in one corner, while in another corner, a teen is using your button-maker to create his next masterpiece. A toddler explores your collection of musical instruments for kids, while a visiting speaker's voice booms from the meeting room. It's a beautiful scene . . . unless you're actually trying to get work done.

Small, rural librarians often aren't lucky enough to have desks that are set away from the chaos of the library—you may not have an office or even a desk of your own. So there you sit behind the circulation desk, surrounded by a continuous onslaught of interruptions, trying to tune out the noise so you can finish up the budget for next year. Most librarians aren't allowed to come in to work when the library is closed—there's just no budget for it—so you must get your work done during open hours or volunteer your time.

Demands at home. Once you go home for the day, chances are your work isn't done. The little amount of energy you have left is most likely spent cleaning up the house, caring for children or pets, or spending time with a significant other. There's nothing left for *you,* and when there is, you just want to take a nap or watch Netflix. (Not that there's anything wrong with that.) You only have so much of yourself to go around, and often there is not much left when you get home from work. Our own personal lives can impede our ability to do a great job at work, so we take our work home with us, which then affects our personal lives. It's a vicious cycle, and once you're in it, it can be hard to reignite that passion you used to have for your job. Some other lifestyle factors that could contribute to burnout are poor sleeping or eating habits, poor time management, and a bad work/life balance.

Inability to delegate. There is nothing wrong with asking for help. Read that again. Repeat it to yourself every single day. You won't win any medals for trying to do everything on your own, and you should not be a martyr to your occupation! Individuals who struggle with delegating are much more susceptible to burnout simply because they take everything on by themselves.

Inability to say no. "Sure, I can take that on," you say with a tight smile, knowing perfectly well that you cannot, in fact, take another thing on. Does that sound familiar? Saying "no" to anything can be difficult when you are constantly having to justify your job or the existence of your library, whether it's to your city, community members, or the national government. You might feel that saying "no" would be to disappoint your community, that piling yet another hat on top of the precariously teetering stack already atop your head will end up being a good idea in the long run. Not so! Learning to say no is one of the most important strategies to avoid burning out. Some other personality factors that can contribute to burnout are perfectionism, pessimism, and having a Type A or high-achieving personality.

TIPS TO AVOID BURNOUT

So maybe you've read the above and found that more than a few things in it ring true for you, and you've come to the conclusion that you are, indeed, on the fast track to burning out. What should you do? Can you avoid it? The answer is yes! With a few self-care tips and strategies for balancing your work with your personal life, it is possible to avoid going any further down the path to job burnout, and bring joy back into your workplace.

Separate library from home. Stop taking work home with you. It's hard to do—you probably go home with your mind full of library-related problems: you respond to e-mails on your days off, you stay up late worrying about those kids who always come into your library barefoot and hungry, you read blurbs about the seventeenth Danielle Steel novel to come out this year and wonder if you really need to order it for the library. (You do. You always do.)

Even though the library is probably always in the back of your mind, it's so important to unplug on your days off and try to forget about it. Your job is incredibly important, it's true . . . but it's not neurosurgery—no one is going to die if you don't respond to that e-mail right this very second. Your home should be designated as a no-work zone—otherwise, you'll never be able to get away from work and will be in danger of it totally overrunning your life. Set boundaries—no phone calls or e-mails after 7:00 p.m., no working from home on weekends, whatever works best for you—and stick to them.

Find people you trust and can depend on, and lean on them hard when you're feeling burned out. Trying to do everything yourself is a surefire way to get burned out. You must remember that you have library assistants for a reason, and it's literally their job to help you. Even if you don't have a library assistant or another staff member, there are likely many people in town who would be happy to help with summer reading or big events. If you're feeling stressed out or overwhelmed, find someone who can help—don't be a hero! You're no good to anyone if you burn yourself out, and it benefits your library and community when you don't bear every burden yourself.

Join discussion lists and Facebook groups—you'll find plenty of librarians who are having the same struggles you're having, and it's always nice to have someone to commiserate right along with you. Try to keep connected with your colleagues. If you can't afford to join an association or attend a conference, contact your state library—they might have grants you could apply for, or have some other ideas on how you can keep in close contact with other small or rural librarians. If your state doesn't provide much for small library support, contact other libraries in your area and create your own little group. If other libraries in communities near you feel isolated as well, get together to do a staff and board networking event for multiple small or rural libraries; you can each bring food to share and talk about your shared struggles and successes. And you get bonus points if you can find a mentor—someone whom you admire in the field whom you can talk openly with, commiserate with, and bounce ideas off of. Having even just one person who knows what you're going through can make a world of difference to a small or rural librarian.

Focus on the positive. It's far too easy to get down on yourself and ruminate on the negative. *I'm horrible at my job. I can't come up with anything new and interesting. I'm not good enough.* Stop doing this! All that will accomplish is to lead you further down the path to burnout. Keep a folder (whether it's physical or on your laptop) full of things that make you happy. Fill it with joy: memes that make you laugh, cute cat photos, pictures of friends and family, and blog posts or articles about the amazing things that libraries do.

Try practicing gratitude each and every day. It sounds corny, but keeping a "gratitude journal" can make a huge difference in your overall attitude. Just one sentence a day about something you're grateful for, and you'll start noticing a change in your outlook. Find those moments of joy, calm, and quiet wherever you can—a peaceful moment at the front desk in between patron questions, an especially successful program, an unexpected compliment from a patron—and celebrate them.

Start a list—in a Word document, in a notebook, or just a random scrap of paper—of positive feedback and compliments you've received from your community, board members, and staff, as well as examples of accomplishments that you're especially proud of. Keep that list handy all the time, and look back at it when you feel down or uninspired. Remember all of the great things you and your library have done, and stop devaluing yourself—know that you are doing a great job, and your community is lucky to have you. Yes, you!

Get outside. Getting out of the library can work wonders when you're having a not-so-great day. Take a walk outside on your lunch break—fresh air is often a cure-all for a case of the blues. If you're lucky enough to get breaks, vacations, and sick days, *take them* if you're starting to feel burned out. Several studies have shown that workers who actually take their vacation time are much more productive, and those who use their sick time come back even more invigorated and have more to give. Everyone needs to take a step back sometimes, and there's absolutely no shame in taking a break. (And when you're on your work breaks, don't forget to eat and drink. Getting dehydrated or "hangry" may not cause burnout, but it sure can be at the root of a terrible day!)

In today's society, "hustling" and being a "boss babe" are praised and idolized. Saying that you "live at the office" seems to be more of a boast these days than a complaint. This is unhealthy. Being constantly tired and exhausted is not proof that you're good at your job and passionate about what you do— it's a red flag that something is wrong and needs to change. It shouldn't be the norm to work through lunch or pull an all-nighter at work. You and your health come before work; don't ever forget that!

Tidy your workspace. Clear up that clutter! A cluttered desk can lead to a cluttered mind. You just can't feel zen when you're surrounded by stacks of papers and new books that need to be processed! Once your desk is clear and organized, you will literally feel your body unclench and relax a little. If you're a bit of a pack-rat, try to tidy your desk just once a day, and pay attention to how good it makes you feel. Make your workspace a happy place, and you'll be so much more productive.

Find your "thing." Find a hobby that has absolutely nothing to do with your work, and do it often! And there are bonus points if your hobby of choice is mindless and relaxing, because then it can be used to unwind after a long, stressful day at work as well. Take a bath, meditate, exercise, cross-stitch, do whatever enables you to chill the most. Learn a new skill and expand your mind. When you're not at work, read only for *pleasure*, not for research. Find what you're passionate about—*besides* the library—and pour yourself into it.

Acknowledge the fact that you are not a superhero. Give yourself permission to do less. You can't possibly do everything all on your own, and it's important to say "no" to things that you simply can't take on. You don't *have* to visit every single preschool classroom—just visit one. You don't need to have a program every day of the week—your patrons will be much happier with one complete, well-thought-out program a week than five rushed, thrown-together ones.

Prioritize and don't be afraid to put less important things on the back burner.

Sometimes in this field of work, there is an unspoken understanding that you will make personal sacrifices in order to better serve the needs of your community. You don't go on vacations in the summer because that's summer reading time, and it should be all hands on deck. You don't call in sick a few days before your big annual fundraiser because your staff can't do it without you, even if you're coughing up a lung. And you'd better not complain about burnout, because don't you love your job? Don't you want to provide amazing services to the community?

This way of thinking is unhealthy and not okay. You must do what you need to do to take care of yourself. Self-care is important, but you also need to make sure that the place you're working in cares for you. It doesn't help to try and avoid burnout if the very place you're working has rules in place that practically encourage it. A good workplace supports its employees, and if you suspect the problem is not in you, but in the institution, it might be time to start looking for a different place to work. Librarians are not superheroes, and they shouldn't be expected to live up to that label.

If you're struggling and on the road to job burnout, take some time for yourself and try some of these tips. One thing to remember is that some symptoms of burnout mirror the symptoms of other, more serious issues. If your exhaustion, lack of interest, irritability, and lack of energy seem chronic and immune to the strategies put forth in this chapter, get yourself to a medical professional. Burnout carries many of the same symptoms as clinical depression, and a doctor can help you distinguish between the two. Self-care does not replace mental health care!

A Note on the Term Self-Care

These days, when you hear the word *self-care*, you might think of fancy face masks, spa retreats, and massages. Although this can all be part of self-care, it doesn't have to be. Self-care doesn't have to cost any money at all—it can be as simple as eating a green leafy vegetable, turning off your phone, or getting eight full hours of uninterrupted sleep. All of these things are important self-care methods that don't cost anything. While pampering yourself with skin-care products or going on a beach vacation are great ways to unwind, it's not all about spending money on frivolous things, and it's far from a selfish act. Self-care is, quite simply, putting on your own oxygen mask before helping others, and it's something that anyone who works in a service profession should be practicing on a day-to-day basis.

RELIGHT YOUR PROGRAMMING FIRE
WITH ONLINE INSPIRATION!

One of the most helpful tips for avoiding or recovering from job burnout and getting your library mojo back is finding inspiration. Sometimes all it takes is a sudden burst of inspiration and excitement about a really cool program idea to get you out of your funk. This can make all the difference when it comes to losing your motivation and passion for programming. Keep a physical list of the websites, blogs, or other places that inspire you, or keep a bookmarks tab on your computer. There are so many blogs, websites, and webinars out there that it can be hard to know where to start. The following are some of my go-tos.

The Old Faithfuls

The Old Faithfuls are tried-and-true websites that aren't specific to library programming. While they aren't library-related, they usually have the latest on what is new and trendy in pop culture and beyond. These sites can also spark ideas for displays or programs.

Pinterest. Pinterest is a crafter's mecca! Type any craft supply or idea into Pinterest, and you'll be bombarded with more ideas than you know what to do with. Pinterest is also rife with easy children's activities, recipes, early literacy information, and organization tips.

Bustle. This site is full of interesting and well-written articles about everything from the royal family to makeup tips. Bustle also posts some great booklists, articles about what's most popular in pop culture, and lists of bookish, literary gifts.

Buzzfeed. This is similar to Bustle, but is aimed at a younger age group. Buzzfeed has tons of video content, listicles, and quizzes on all sorts of pop culture. The site also posts tons of yummy recipes and helpful tips for everything from holiday decorating to self-care tips.

Book Riot. On this site you can find literary gifts, booklists and reviews, lots of great discussion on diversity in books, and even a few articles on working in libraries.

PopSugar Books (popsugar.com/books). On this site you can browse through countless lists of books curated by topic or genre—climate change, medical thrillers, trans/nonbinary authors, the list goes on. There are also roundups of great literary products, and articles on banned books on the site.

Google Trends (trends.google.com). Get an idea of what's "popular" by poking around on the Google Trends page, which lists the most popular searches of the day and year. These can come in handy when you feel a bit out of the loop and want to create an of-the-moment program or display.

Disney Family (family.disney.com). This family-friendly site includes lots of crafts, recipes, and activities that a Disney-obsessed parent can do with their child.

Crafty Blogs

Again, these sites aren't library-related, but they include a great assortment of ideas for craft, event, and program planning.

Kara's Party Ideas (karaspartyideas.com/blog). This is technically a party-planning blog, but you will be inspired by the beautiful photography featured on the page. Kara is considered to be the Martha Stewart of the event-planning world, and she has been featured as a Michael's Maker for Michael's stores and is a stylist for the Oriental Trading website. Did the summer reading theme "A Universe of Stories" leave you feeling uninspired? Search "aliens," "outer space," or "galaxy" on this blog, and you'll be overwhelmed by all the beautiful décor, snack ideas, and game and craft ideas that pop up. Browse through her page when you're feeling blah about program planning, and you'll walk away with so many new ideas, from a Mother's Day tea party to a kid-friendly version of Coachella.

Hands On as We Grow (handsonaswegrow.com). Looking for toddler-friendly craft ideas? Or maybe you need a fun science experiment for grade-school kids? From art projects and sensory bins to learning games and innovative holiday crafts, it's all on this blog. The author is a mom with three young boys who started the blog to help other busy parents who needed something fun and creative to keep their kids' hands and minds occupied. You can browse by age or subject, and my favorite part of the site is the search bar—if you find yourself with an abundance of felt, for example, just type the word "felt" into the search bar, and you won't believe how many projects come up!

Infarrantly Creative (infarrantlycreative.net). You can find just about any craft on this site, but it's geared toward adult crafts rather than ones for kids. There are even some fun, easy recipes mixed in, as well as some holiday décor ideas.

Fabulous in First (fabulousinfirst.com). A first-grade teacher posts about various classroom ideas, literacy information, and book lists on this fun blog. Many of the things she does in her classroom—karaoke, camping day—would be easy to replicate at a library.

Fun in First (funinfirst.com). Very similar is the *Fun in First* blog, which includes worksheets and coloring pages, roundups of toys and products, and unique organization ideas, all of which can be used at a public library.

Library Blogs

Though the list of blogs written by public librarians could go for pages and pages, here are just a few that are sure to be helpful to you when planning programs. Don't forget to go through the archives if they aren't up-to-date, and check out these blogs' home pages for lists of even more recommended blogs!

Letters to a Young Librarian (letterstoayounglibrarian.blogspot.com). This blog is now defunct, but its archives are pure gold. They're chock-full of interviews with various talented individuals working in libraries and helpful posts on everything from being a good boss to surviving tasks that you don't enjoy. This blog is worth a look.

Programming Librarian (programminglibrarian.org/blogs). You've probably already heard of this one, but this site is focused solely on programming in libraries of all sizes. You can narrow your search to showing only free ideas for rural libraries, so it makes your brainstorming super-easy. This site is lucky to have some *very* talented bloggers writing for it. (I'm a little biased.)

Abby the Librarian (abbythelibrarian.com). This blog is very kid-centric and has amazing ideas for summer reading and science programs, along with some great book recommendations.

ALSC Blog (alsc.ala.org/blog). The Association for Library Service to Children runs this blog, which features posts about youth programming as well as news that affects the world of youth librarians. You can learn about diversity in children's books and read about how to plan a stuffed animal sleepover.

The Neighborhood Librarian (neighborhoodlibrarian.com). Blogger Brytani loves rural libraries and writes some beautiful posts about librarianship. Though the blog is dormant, you can still browse through her archives to learn about putting on a Goosebumps party or doing awesome outreach events.

Teen Services Underground (teenservicesunderground.com). This blog focuses solely on programming for teens. It has tons of posts on things like inclusivity, putting on a comic-con, and the best social media platform to use to reach teens.

In Short, I Am Busy (inshortbusy.blogspot.com). Jean the librarian shares all of her programming "recipes" along with her daily schedule on this blog. She discusses outreach, makerspaces, art workshops, and so much more.

Hafuboti (hafuboti.com). Rebecca is an outspoken and super-creative librarian in Nebraska. She shares her display ideas, and décor and program examples on this very fun blog. Don't forget to browse through her archives!

Literacious (literacious.com). This beautiful, easy-to-navigate blog features themed book lists, ways to spread kindness in your library, book-themed parties, and more!

5 Min. Librarian (5minlib.com). This is a super-helpful blog full of lists relevant to those who work in the library world. Their specialty seems to be themed book display ideas, but they also talk about hot tips for libraries on Facebook, holiday programming alternatives, and why graphic novels *are* real books.

Jbrary (jbrary.com). Lindsey and Dana are the two children's librarians behind *Jbrary*, and they also run their own YouTube channel. Their emphasis is storytime and everything that entails—fingerplays, songs, flannel boards, and more.

Lightsome Librarian (lightsomelibrarian.blogspot.com). This is an amazing resource for storytime themes, with everything included!

Storytime Katie (storytimekatie.com). This is another great resource for storytime themes, plus outreach ideas and crafts.

Super Library Marketing (superlibrarymarketing.com). Angela Hursh is a well-known marketing librarian, and she shares her expertise on various ways to advertise your library.

S. Bryce Kozla (brycekozlablog.blogspot.com). You can find a little bit of everything on this outspoken librarian's blog—serious posts on diversity and inclusivity, light-hearted posts on summer reading and outreach, plus a great sense of humor!

Teen Services Depot (teenservicesdepot.wordpress.com). Dawn is a teen services coordinator in Illinois, and it's clear from her blog how passionate she is about programming for teens. Learn how to do everything from a K-Pop party to teen book box subscriptions, to creating a makerspace from scratch!

Fat Girl Reading (fatgirlreading.com). Angie Manfredi is now the youth services consultant for the State Library of Iowa, and we're lucky to have her! Her blog archives are amazing—my particular favorites are "Dinosaurs @ Your Library!" and the series of posts on how she refreshed her library's summer reading program.

The Loudmouth Librarian (theloudmouthlibrarian.com). Lots of great teen programming ideas can be found in this blog's archives.

Ontarian Librarian (ontarianlibrarian.com). Book displays, program ideas, and reader's advisory tools can all be found here. You can find ideas that apply to patrons of any age, not just kids.

Useful Library Webinars

There's nothing better than a really helpful webinar. The best are the ones that just hit you with program idea after program idea, and you end up with pages of notes. There are a lot of them out there, but these are some of the best; you'll have to register for some of them, but they're all free to watch or listen to.

How to Break Up Boredom: Interactive Events for All Ages (WebJunction). This offers exciting programs for patrons of all ages that won't break the bank—what more could you ask for?

From Tots to Teens: STEAM-Powered Ideas for Programming (WebJunction). Whether you're a STEAM expert or aren't even sure what the letters stand for, this webinar will help you to plan enriching programs for kids from preschool age to teenagers.

Adult Programs on a $0 Budget (WebJunction). Planning successful adult programs can be tough, but this presentation makes it easy to turn your library into the hub of the community.

Bigger on the Inside: Programming for Small Spaces (Programming Librarian). No matter how tiny your library building is, it's possible to pull off amazing events that maximize the space you have—this webinar shows you how!

Size Doesn't Matter: Transforming Big Ideas into Small Library Environments (Programming Librarian). If you've ever been at a conference and thought,

"That would never work at my library," you're in luck! This webinar shows you how it's possible to re-create large-scale programs in a small library.

Steal These Ideas!

Join a discussion list. These are a form of passive mentorship that you can be added to in order to receive and share great ideas with others in your field. The American Library Association website has a long list of discussion lists with various focuses.

Join a Facebook group. Facebook groups like Library Think Tank, Programming Librarian Interest Group, and Tiny Library Think Tank can be invaluable when it comes to seeking advice from other librarians.

Listen to a podcast. A few podcasts were mentioned in the chapter on marketing, but here are a few more: Storytime Out Loud is a podcast all about storytime themes, Adventures in YA explores young adult literature, and Circulating Ideas facilitates conversations about the innovative people who help libraries thrive.

Incorporate your hobbies. Bringing your own hobbies into the library can be a great way to create successful programs. If you're passionate about animal rescue, partner up with your local humane society. Are you really amazing at knitting? Create a knitting club at your library. When you're excited about a program, chances are it will be a success. Think about what *you* would like to see offered at the library if you were a patron, and go from there.

Look through publishers' catalogs. Browse through publishers' catalogs to see all the new titles that will be coming out. If there's a lot of books on one specific topic, it's probably going to be a trend, and it's time for your library to jump on the bandwagon!

Attend a conference. If your library can afford it, go to as many library conferences and meetings as you can. The Association for Rural & Small Libraries conference is particularly helpful for little libraries, and you'll end up going home with a notebook chock-full of notes and ideas. Librarians often walk away from conferences feeling refreshed and reinvigorated, and can see their library with clear eyes. If the travel costs aren't in your budget, look around for grants and scholarships that would allow you to attend.

Read an ALA publication. Again, I might be a little biased here, but library-focused books are a godsend for librarians who need some inspiration. If you'd rather not purchase any of these books, many of them can be found at your state library or through interlibrary loan.

Visit a craft or hobby store. Who knows what you might come across when walking through the aisles of Hobby Lobby or a similar store? Maybe you'll come across a rock-painting kit that inspires you to try it as a program, or you might find some really amazing beads that you decide to use in a jewelry-making class.

Check out local bookstores. Even though your library probably doesn't have the funding to have displays as elaborate as those in bookstores, featuring multiple copies of every single book, you can still pull ideas from a bookstore. Steal their ideas for displays and décor, and make them work in your library. If a local independent bookstore is especially involved in their community, they might have events that you can draw inspiration from as well. There is a children's bookstore in Monroe, Georgia, called The Story Shop that is such a delight—there is a book ladder, a Harry Potter-themed room, and even a Hobbit hole and a yellow brick road!

Visit other libraries. Librarians are usually very excited to share their ideas with other libraries. Make a point to stop by other local libraries and see what they're up to. If you're on an out-of-state trip, stop by a library there and see how their programs differ from yours.

Feeling inspired yet? Get out there and program!

Conclusion

Little Libraries Are Powerful Libraries

ONE OF THE BIG TAKEAWAYS FROM THIS BOOK SHOULD BE JUST
how important public libraries are to their communities, especially in small
towns. Libraries bring people together, and that matters now more than ever.
Communities need libraries for the amazing services they provide, and libraries need as much support as they can get in order to survive and thrive. Small,
rural libraries are the lifeblood of their community, and the people who staff
them do wonders in bringing creativity, vitality, and *life* to the town.

FINAL THOUGHTS ON SMALL-TOWN LIBRARIANSHIP

Rural libraries need leaders like you. There is a phenomenon that researchers call
the "graying" of librarianship, meaning that leaders in small, rural libraries
who have been there for years are reaching the age when they would like to
retire. The vacant positions they leave aren't usually very appealing to young
professionals because these libraries typically can't offer much for pay—it's
not in the budget. So these jobs sometimes go to people who just need a
job, who aren't necessarily passionate about working in a library, and a ton
of potential might go to waste. Rural libraries need strong leaders who are
excited about the work they do. They need people who love people, and who
take pleasure in helping revitalize their community. Sure, the salaries might

be low, but a dollar goes a lot further in a small town, and housing costs are usually reasonable. Experiencing the rewards of working in a small library and seeing the community change right before your eyes as a result of something *you* helped do will be worth it.

You can do anything, but you can't do everything all at once. If you're just starting in a small library and thinking of making some major changes, slow down and take a beat. Little towns can be wary of new people with new ideas, and you don't want to bulldoze your way into the community. You want to spend some time listening and gathering feedback from community members before trying to change everything. Trust is important, so get out there and get involved, and if you're getting a lot of pushback on a change you're trying to make, drop it for now and revisit it at a later date. Choose your battles wisely, and remember that being a small librarian is all about relationships. When you do decide to start making changes, don't go it alone—ask for help and invite your patrons and the city council to share their feedback.

Don't be afraid to brag. Celebrate your successes, and boast about your library when you can. If no one knows about that great thing your library did, did it really even happen?

Numbers don't matter as much as you think they do. There is so much more to a small library than numbers. Circulation and program participation numbers matter, certainly, but what matters the most is how your community is responding to the library. Are you meeting their needs? Do they enjoy the services you offer? Do they feel at home when they are at the library? If the answer to these questions is yes, you're doing just fine. You can measure a library's success in many ways.

Partnerships can make all the difference. Partnerships are key to a rural or small library's success, so get out there and ask. Publicly acknowledge everyone who helped, and nurture those relationships. A library is most successful when there's reciprocity, an active back-and-forth relationship between it and the community.

Serve everyone. Don't buy books or plan programs solely for the majority. Your program offerings and materials selection should be diverse and inclusive, and the library should be a community melting pot of sorts. Anyone should be able to walk into your library and find a book that they can relate to and see themselves reflected in. Libraries are for everyone, not *most* everyone.

Be a good human. If you don't like people, you probably shouldn't work in a rural or small library. As the face of your library, be sure you're always treating everyone with kindness—greet people when they come in the door, and thank them when they leave. Make every library-related interaction positive, whether you're inside the building or not. Be grateful for the good things about your job—take joy in what you *do* have rather than being sad about what you don't. What you take for granted in your library, other libraries might treasure. Continue to grow professionally through conferences and continuing education, regardless of how long you've been working in libraries, so your attitude when it comes to work stays fresh and invigorated. Remember why you are doing this, and remember how important it is.

It's okay not to have an MLIS degree. This is a tough subject in the library world. It has to do with the use of the word *librarian*, and whether or not you have to have a master's degree in library science to be called one. You don't have to have a library degree to be successful at what you do. A degree is a very expensive piece of paper, and it doesn't automatically make you good at your job. Getting your MLIS is not the *only* path to librarianship, and it often just isn't very realistic when it comes to working in a small, rural library.

Reach out to those who need you. If you are employed by a large library in a less rural area, check in on the librarians you know in small libraries who might be struggling. If you attended a conference that they weren't able to go to, share your notes from the presentations. Go out of your way to help lift them up and see what they need.

What you do is important, and you—your mind, your creativity, your capacity to create amazing and impactful programs—are so needed in the field of librarianship. No matter how tiny your library is, it is absolutely vital to your community. I hope this book has left you feeling inspired and ready to jump into programming with both feet. You're already doing amazing things, and your community can't wait to see what you come up with next!

Appendix

Where to Find Grants

Lists of Grant Opportunities

Scholastic—scholastic.com/librarians/programs/grants.htm

American Library Association—ala.org/awardsgrants

Association for Library Service to Children—ala.org/alsc/awardsgrants

Young Adult Library Services Association—ala.org/yalsa/awardsandgrants/yalsaawardsgrants

Public Library Association—ala.org/pla/awards

Directories

GrantWatch—grantwatch.com

GrantStation—grantstation.com

The Grantsmanship Center—tgci.com

Candid—candid.org

Foundation Center—libraries.foundationcenter.org

Grants.gov

Library Grants—librarygrants.blogspot.com

GuideStar—guidestar.org

Foundations

Dollar General Literacy Foundation—dgliteracy.org

Walmart—walmart.org/how-we-give

Target—corporate.target.com/corporate-responsibility/philanthropy

Home Depot—corporate.homedepot.com/foundation/grants

Costco—costco.com/charitable-giving.html

Ezra Jack Keats Foundation—ezra-jack-keats.org/section/ezra-jack
-keats-mini-grant-program-for-public-libraries-public-schools/

The Pilcrow Foundation—thepilcrowfoundation.org

Better World Books—cares.betterworldbooks.com/grants

Community or county foundations

Federal/Government

Institute of Museum and Library Services—imls.gov/grants/grant
-programs

National Endowment for the Humanities—neh.gov/grants

U.S. Department of Education—www2.ed.gov/programs/find/elig/
index.html

LSTA grant through your state

United Way grant through your county or state government

Other Sources

Local banks

Local realtors

Local cultural council grants

Local clubs: Lions, Rotary, Kiwanis

Aldi—corporate.aldi.us/en/corporate-responsibility/community/
local-grants/

Fareway—fareway.com/about/community-outreach

Hy-Vee—hy-vee.com/corporate/our-company/community/charitable
-donations/

Index